"Those who carry the cross of Christ to the farthest reaches of the Himalayas will find that in some villages there are no girls over the age of twelve. Gerhardt helps us make sense of the maddening global violence against women and girls by providing a theological response—a heartening call to live out the confession of our faith. From the foot of the cross, she challenges us to identify with those who suffer as we bind up the brokenhearted and set the oppressed free. In *The Cross and Gendercide*, the church is urged to elevate the discussion beyond proclamation versus social action to what Bonhoeffer described as a faith that gives us the courage to take risks as we bring good news in all its fullness to those in peril. Read this book and then join the resistance of the greatest injustice of our century: the wholesale abuse and exploitation of women and girls."

Michele M. Rickett, president and founder of She Is Safe and coauthor of *Forgotten Girls*

The CROSS and GENDERCIDE

A Theological Response to Global Violence Against Women and Girls

ELIZABETH GERHARDT

IVP Academic

An imprint of InterVarsity Press
Downers Grove, Illinois

InterVarsity Press
P.O. Box 1400, Downers Grove, IL 60515-1426
World Wide Web: www.ivpress.com
Email: email@ivpress.com

InterVarsity Press® is the book-publishing division of InterVarsity Christian Fellowship/USA®, a movement of students and faculty active on campus at hundreds of universities, colleges and schools of nursing in the United States of America, and a member movement of the International Fellowship of Evangelical Students. For information about local and regional activities, write Public Relations Dept., InterVarsity Christian Fellowship/USA, 6400 Schroeder Rd., P.O. Box 7895, Madison, WI 53707-7895, or visit the IVCF website at www.intervarsity.org.

Scripture quotations, unless otherwise noted, are from the New Revised Standard Version of the Bible, copyright 1989 by the Division of Christian Education of the National Council of the Churches of Christ in the USA. Used by permission. All rights reserved.

While all stories in this book are true, some names and identifying information in this book have been changed to protect the privacy of the individuals involved.

Cover design: Cindy Kiple
Interior design: Beth Hagenberg
Images: Cyndi Monaghan/Getty Images

ISBN 978-0-8308-4049-6 (print)
ISBN 978-0-8308-8022-5 (digital)

Printed in the United States of America ∞

Library of Congress Cataloging-in-Publication Data

A catalog record for this book is available from the Library of Congress.

P	22	21	20	19	18	17	16	15	14	13	12	11	10	9	8	7	6	5	4	3	2	1
Y	33	32	31	30	29	28	27	26	25	24	23	22	21	20	19	18	17	16	15	14		

CONTENTS

ACKNOWLEDGMENTS

This book could never have been written without the support and expertise of many others. For over twenty-five years I have had the privilege of listening to the stories of hundreds of women and girls who are survivors of many forms of violence. Their courage and strength have inspired and taught me about the triumph of grace and love. I am indebted to them for their willingness to share their experiences with me. Their names are anonymous, but their stories have shaped my understanding of both the causes of violence and its solutions.

I could not have created the space and time to work on this research without the benefit of a sabbatical that was generously granted by the administration and board of Roberts Wesleyan College and Northeastern Seminary. In particular, special thanks go to Dr. Douglas Cullum, dean of Northeastern Seminary; Drs. Richard Middleton and Rebecca Letterman, colleagues who offered their support; and especially Dr. David Basinger, who provided encouragement throughout the project.

I want to thank InterVarsity Press, particularly David Congdon, who generously guided this work by his editorial expertise. And I offer a very special thank you and acknowledgment to my friend Niki Brodeur, who provided feedback and reference editing, with humor and great patience.

This book most certainly would not have been possible without the knowledge, teaching and scholarship of my mentor, Dr. Carter Lindberg. Carter's passion for Luther's theology and his deeply thoughtful insights on the implications for contemporary social ethics continue to inspire me. Though I have not been his student for many years, I continue to learn from his work, which has been foundational for my own research, teaching and writing.

Finally, this book is dedicated to my beloved daughter, Virginia Joy Mei. Her deep curiosity, joy and presence act as a daily reminder that love is found in the sacred ordinariness of living.

Abbreviations

LW   *Luther's Works*. Edited by Jaroslav Pelikan (vols. 1-30) and Helmut T. Lehmann (vols. 31-55). St. Louis: Concordia, 1968–.

DBWE   *Dietrich Bonhoeffer Works—English Edition*. 16 vols. Minneapolis: Fortress, 2003–2013.

Things do exist that are worth standing up for without compromise.
To me it seems that peace and social justice are such things,
as is Christ himself.

DIETRICH BONHOEFFER

- 1 -

A Point of Departure

The Cross and Global Violence
Against Women and Girls

LINDA WALKED TENTATIVELY into my small basement office. She was a young woman with short-cropped hair and a fresh, newly stitched wound that stretched from her temple, ran across her cheek and ended at her chin. Linda related her terrifying story with little affect and trembling hand gestures. "My husband chased me around the house with a butcher knife and caught up to me, slashing me in my arm and face." She rolled up her sleeve to show me more stitches. "I ran out of the house screaming, and my neighbor called the police." Linda's face finally began to mirror the pain in her voice, and she began to sob. "The policeman walked across the lawn, looked down on me and asked me what I had done to deserve my husband's abuse." She pointed to her cheek, "I feel like I've been victimized twice, first by my husband and second by the police!" Linda was my first client and my first introduction to the shadow world of violence against women and girls. Over the years I heard hundreds of stories from battered women and girls. Through each story I learned more of the cultural, religious, historical and political supports for violence and the global scope of these heinous crimes.

Violence against women and girls is a human rights problem that impacts the lives of millions of families and communities. In the United States one out of every four women has experienced domestic violence and one out of six has experienced attempted or completed rape. Almost one and a half million women have been abused during the past year, and the health costs are an astounding 5.8 billion dollars.[1] Violence against women has been identified as the leading cause of injury to women between the ages of fifteen and forty-nine[2] and is one of the country's most expensive health problems.[3] Globally, it is a significant and complex human rights problem that exacerbates the problems of poverty, child abandonment, communicable diseases and homelessness. The perception of violence as a private, family problem has obscured efforts to increase the visibility of this dilemma as a public human rights issue that affects all members of society. Violence against women and girls crosses all borders, cultures and classes.[4]

Statistics that provide a snapshot of the extent of this global problem are overwhelming. Although prohibited in most countries, violence continues and is permitted by political, social and religious institutions and systems and remains the major cause of the most violent attacks on women and girls. Global violence against women and girls takes on many forms: widespread rape as a tool of war, gender-selective abortions, female genital mutilation, sexual trafficking, disfigurement and economic exploitation of women, among other horrific violent crimes. Maymuna, a fifteen-year-old Nigerian girl, was forced into marrying a sixty-five-year-old local man. She conceived three months later. Her labor lasted for days before she was taken to a hospital that was three hours away. By the time she arrived, her uterus had ruptured, and she

---

[1]Statistics have been compiled by the National Coalition Against Domestic Violence, accessed June 27, 2013, www.ncadv.org/files/DomesticViolenceFactSheet(National).pdf.

[2]World Health Organization, *Violence Against Women: Fact Sheet No. 239*, November 2012, www.who .int/mediacentre/factsheets/fs239/en/index.html.

[3]Phil B. Fontanarosa, "The Unrelenting Epidemic of Violence in America: Truths and Consequences," *Journal of the American Medical Association* 273 (1995): 1792-93.

[4]The Women's Rights Network (WRN) was founded in 1995 in Boston to provide a central international clearinghouse and educational center on this issue of domestic violence as an international human rights issue. Only in the past three years have human rights organizations begun to examine the problem of domestic violence as both an international and a human rights issue using the Universal Declaration of Human Rights as an educational tool. Domestic violence is not considered a crime in many countries, and where it is illegal, the laws are often not enforced. For more information, see the Amnesty International publication *It's About Time! Human Rights Are Women's Rights* (New York: Amnesty International USA, 1995).

struggled to survive. As a result of hemorrhaging, both she and her baby died. Maymuna's tragic story is one among tens of thousands illustrating this one type of violence and exploitation.[5]

In recent years nongovernmental organizations (NGOs), governmental bodies and other agencies have been effective in bringing attention to this critical problem. Christian churches also contribute in several ways to the prevention and elimination of "gendercide."[6] Efforts include identifying and describing the problem, working to educate Christians as to the extent of the problem, encouraging support to victims, and philanthropic efforts to aid women and girls in need. And yet, there is often a halting acknowledgment by churches to identify violence against women and girls as a theological and confessional issue that requires a unified, holistic church response. The underlying causes of global violence against women and girls are rooted deep in our cultures, and the scandal of this violence is symptomatic of a pervasive and deep misogyny. Millions of girls have undergone the brutal practice of female genital mutilation. Millions of women been forced to undergo sex-selective abortions. Millions more have experienced the horror of sex trafficking and have been imprisoned as slaves with no hope of escape. The list of reprehensible acts is long, and the targets are primarily girls and women. The stubborn pervasiveness of this violence and its deep rootedness in misogyny is best defined as a theological issue, rather than merely an ethical or moral issue. Christian confession concerns an orientation that begins with our understanding of the being of God and subsequently, God's mission in the world. By using this theological approach, the church can offer a broad, imaginative and effective response.

Pulitzer Prize winners and *New York Times* journalists Nicholas D.

---

[5]Chioma Obinna, "Nigeria: Safe Motherhood—Need for Access to Quality Prenatal and Delivery Services," *Vanguard*, February 17, 2012, http://allafrica.com/stories/201202170824.html.

[6]Nicholas Kristof and Sheryl WuDunn define violence against women and children as "gendercide" in their book *Half the Sky: Turning Oppression into Opportunities for Women Worldwide* (New York: Knopf, 2009). I have adopted this term as the most accurate descriptor of this problem. See my expanded analysis of the term in chapter two, "The Numbers and the Stories: The Extent of the Violence."

Kristof and Sheryl WuDunn sum up the critical issue of exploitation and violence against women and girls:

> The global statistics on the abuse of girls are numbing. It appears that more girls have been killed in the last fifty years, precisely because they were girls, than men were killed in all the battles of the twentieth century. More girls are killed in this routine "gendercide" in any one decade than people were slaughtered in all the genocides of the twentieth century.
>
> In the nineteenth century, the central moral challenge was slavery. In the twentieth century, it was the battle against totalitarianism. We believe that in this century the paramount moral challenge will be the struggle for gender equality around the world.[7]

Kristoff relates the story of a girl named Jackie, a fourteen-year-old teen, who is living in Liberia. Jackie is too young to remember the 1993–2003 civil war in Liberia in which three-fourths of the women were brutally raped. However, rape continues to be a lasting vestige of the horrific violence. Jackie was taken to the beach by a fifty-year-old man working at Jackie's school. There he stripped and raped her and left her sobbing. Unable to walk, she was taken to the hospital and spent weeks recovering as a result of massive hemorrhaging. She now resides in a shelter for sexually abused girls. The shelter supports and provides medical services to children as young as three months old. Jackie's body has healed, but she, like so many other girls and women worldwide, suffer the emotional, spiritual and psychological scars of all forms of sexual abuse.[8]

More than twenty-five years of working with abused women have led me to a deeper understanding of the systemic causes of violence against women and girls. These underlying causes of violence, rooted in misogyny and expressed through patriarchy, domination and the objectification of girls and women, are the same for domestic violence in the home and for all forms of global gendercide. Currently, there are many

---

[7]Ibid., p. xvii.
[8]Nicholas D. Kristof, "After Wars, Mass Rapes Persist," *New York Times,* May 20, 2009, www.nytimes.com/2009/05/21/opinion/21kristof.html.

good published resources that focus on education, counseling and self-help in the area of domestic violence. However, it is important for the church to develop a theologically based response to global violence against women and girls that is faithful to the proclamation of the *whole* gospel of life and is equipped to address the underlying economic, cultural, religious and political causes of the violence.

If the issue of violence against women and girls is defined narrowly as a moral issue, it results in a reactive response and becomes compartmentalized within the church. For example, a church invites a guest speaker to discuss the issue of domestic violence in their community during the month of October (domestic violence month). The overall church response is favorable. There is a decision to set up a committee to focus on how the church can help battered women in their local community. Several women volunteer and engage in outreach to the local shelter, organize donations and perhaps provide financial help. This may be an ongoing committee, or it may be replaced by another "cause" in another two years. This common scenario is played out in many denominations and independent churches throughout the United States every week. Although worthwhile, in terms of the aid offered to local battered-women programs, it is limited because its approach is narrowly conceived as a moral and ethical problem. Therefore, it results in a partial response. The response is focused on consciousness raising and is not rooted in deeper theological reflection that would elicit these questions in the church community: What are the nature and roots of the violence? How is the violence that these women have experienced a symptom of larger cultural, spiritual and economic conditions in our churches and society? How do we respond as a whole church community (and avoid minimizing the issue by sending it to committee)? How does our local church understand the role of women? Do we participate in the subjugation of women by limiting their roles in the church? What do Scripture and our theology teach us regarding an approach toward violence and peacemaking? What concepts, language and orientation does our theology offer to help us shape a cohesive, powerful response to the violence? How is the violence in our local community related to global violence against women and girls? Should we define this as a confessional, broad issue needing a multifaceted approach rather than defining this as a moral issue that is worthy only of being relegated to a small group of interested community members?

I propose that a theology of the cross provides the church with a critical foundation for offering assistance to victims while it works to change systems based on gender inequality. The false dichotomy and ideologically based division of faith and ethics in much of the American church landscape is an impediment to a substantial, unified response to the brutality of the existing global violence against girls and women. The most effective response cannot be reactive and partial; rather, it must be embedded in a theological spirituality of the cross that is imaginative, hopeful and holistic in its response to the critical global problem of violence against girls and women. By embracing a theology of the cross that is, in essence, a theology of faith and mission, we can then apply this to the critical problem of violence against girls and women, and to other related global problems.

Dietrich Bonhoeffer described the role of the church as twofold: proclamation of the gospel (*kerygma*) and service to neighbor (*diakonia*). Historically, few Christians would argue with the assertion that both of these tasks are essential and integral to the Scripture. And yet, Christians are often divided in their views of the relationship between faith and ethics, particularly as interpreted through the lens of American culture and politics. There is division between those that detach Christianity from care for one's neighbor because of an emphasis on the American values of individual freedom and rights, and those that emphasize ethics and the prophetic role of the church in calling for social justice. Layered onto American Christian identity is a tendency to overidentify with political ideologies.

This Christian divide is not unique to our time and American experience. Historically, the church has struggled with the theological issues related to the relationship of faith and ethics. Dietrich Bonhoeffer's question, "Who is Jesus Christ for us today?" is a perennial one and a critical one for the church of the twenty-first century. This theological question and its ecclesiastical counterpoint, "What is the church's role in the world today?" provide a foundation for examining specific issues related to violence against women and girls. Addressing these questions is critical because the Christian church cannot adequately address gender violence while divided over issues related to faith and ethics and the resulting cultural and social policy implications. The theological and spiritual themes related to both *kerygma* and *diakonia* include the meaning of Christian freedom, the role of suffering, the dialectic of faith and works, Christian identification with the poor, and the relationship of church and state. These are the themes that provide a theological foundation for addressing the central issue of our time: global violence against girls and women.

Theology as proclamation of the gospel provides a confession of a God who prohibits idolatry on the basis of a confessional, rather than a pietistic, morality. The underlying problem of a disconnected, reactive church response comes from a lack of clarity of the relationship of *kerygma* and *diakonia*. Churches that emphasize the preaching of the gospel and then ignore the reality of the plight of millions of women and girls are guilty of a detached confessionalism. The ultimate reality of God is then divorced from the penultimate political and social realities of gendercide and its related social problems.

DEFINING THE PROBLEM

There is little or no dispute among conscientious church leaders, academics, political pundits and caring Christians that abuse of women and girls anywhere around the globe is reprehensible. Theoretically, the existing conditions that promote sex trafficking, widespread rape, acid burnings, domestic violence and the suffering of girls forced to undergo genital mutilation are condemned by leaders in both mainline denominations and evangelical independent churches, feminists and conservatives alike. However, abstract understanding and theoretical knowledge do not necessarily mean that the underlying causes of violence and unified practical response to these problems are agreed upon. Layered upon these divisions is a general lack of passionate initiatives to come together and work not only to aid victims of violence but to end systemic political and social supports of gender violence. There are several reasons for this Christian disunity. It is easy to acknowledge that there is a problem of violence directed toward women and girls. However, it is not so easy to accept the prevalence and degree of that violence, and our own complicity in supporting gendercide.

The term *gendercide* is helpful in raising consciousness because it identifies the problem for what it is, an intentional effort to harm and injure millions of women and girls based on their gender. Approximately four million women go "missing" each year in developing countries.[9] There is a systematic effort to oppress and violate women and girls for purposes that are political, financial, religious and social in nature. The obvious connection of the term *gendercide* to other genocides helps underscore the seriousness of the problem and the need for a global response. There is also a level of discomfort in confronting this issue because the statistics are numbing and the personal stories are heartbreaking. It is far too easy for American Christians to shake our heads and sympathize with the victims and then respond by retreating into our comfortable worlds. Writing checks to worthwhile organizations is important, but it is not enough. Churches often respond by having an annual offering for missions, and may go so far as to set up a committee to investigate and study global issues and promote special activities. While this approach may promote good feelings, and the church can argue that it does address justice issues, the reality is that the response is partial and anemic. It doesn't go far enough in its response to the horror of gendercide.

This is not to say that much good work hasn't been done to promote justice, educate church members and financially support worthwhile

---

[9]World Bank, *World Development Report 2012: Gender Equality and Development* (Washington, DC: World Bank Publications, 2011).

global justice-promoting organizations. This happens in mainline, liberal and conservative churches. However, no unified outcry and response to the global problem of gendercide has yet come from church leaders. Their response has been compartmentalized and predominantly centered on individual giving. What is needed is a powerful theological voice for change, the will to become uncomfortable in the face of the realities of women's and girls' lives, and a more Christ-centered response that is also political, social and economic in nature. A theology of the cross provides the right point of departure not only because it is centered on the incarnational saving work of Christ but because it is rooted in the Christian common confession of faith. All Christians share the same baptism in Christ and are unified by faith in the one essential act on the cross. It is from this reference point that Jesus got on his knees and washed the feet of his disciples and commanded them to do the same. It was on the cross that Jesus told John to care for his mother. All concern for preservation of the self dies at the foot of the cross. The gift of freedom for Christians is a freedom *for the other*. All Christians, of every denomination and polity, share this common foundation of faith. The mission of the church is rooted in this central understanding and acceptance of Christ's work on the cross. The hope integral to effective ministry is birthed in the reality of the final work of the cross, resurrection.

From this perspective, the first steps for the whole of the church are to become better educated regarding the extent of the problem, to use theological and legal human rights language to define *gendercide* and, subsequently, to engage in resistance to the cultural, political and religious systems that continue to support this violence. However, it is only a first step. Without a common understanding of the faith and mission of the church, rooted in a theology of the cross, it is difficult to move beyond raised consciousness and theoretical, abstract analysis to a broadened definition of the church's mission that includes violence against women and girls as a confessional issue that needs to be addressed by the *whole* of the Christian church.

PERSISTENT SYSTEMATIC VIOLENCE: THREE SHORT STORIES

The following stories illustrate the complexity of violence against women and girls and the depth of the cultural, religious and economic structural supports for the violence.

Ashmita. Ashmita is not her given name. The fifteen-year-old girl from a central Indian district was given the name Nakusa, meaning "unwanted," by her disappointed grandfather. Ashmita was the name she now chose for herself. It means "very tough" or "rock hard" in Hindi. Ashmita participated in a renaming ceremony for 285 girls from her region. Sudha Kankaria, of the organization Save the Girl Child, reported that these name-changing ceremonies are the beginning of a process to change the girls' feelings from worthlessness and low status in the community to dignity and acceptance.[10] Activists claim that Nakusa, or "unwanted," is a name that burdens girls all over India.

This name reflects the plight of Indian girls in a culture that favors sons over daughters. Families often go into debt arranging marriages and paying for dowries. The 2011 census revealed that the nation's sex ratio had dropped over the past decade from 927 girls for every 1,000 boys under the age of six to 914 girls. Some districts report an even greater discrepancy. In the district of Satara, for example, it is even lower, at 881 to 1,000. Such ratios are the result of abortions of female fetuses or sheer neglect, resulting in a higher death rate among girls.[11] Girls are also sold to other countries, to be used for labor or the sex trade. Ashmita's chances for new life are more hopeful than those of millions of other girls. Her name, "unwanted," was changed to symbolize the beginning of a new life for her. There are millions of other girls in Asia, Africa and throughout the world who are unwanted. They remain at risk without intervention.

Lindy. We first met fifteen-year-old Lindy outside a newly built orphanage near Fushun, China, close to the North Korean border. She

---

[10]Chaya Babu, "285 Indian Girls Shed 'Unwanted' Names," *Guardian,* October 22, 2011, www.guardian
  .co.uk/world/feedarticle/9908439.
[11]Ibid.

introduced herself through our translator and shyly asked if Virginia, my twelve-year-old daughter, would like to see her room. The scene could have taken place anywhere in the United States where two young girls first become friends. However, Lindy's "bedroom" was a room filled with two rows of twelve thin single mattresses on wooden frames. There were no dressers, no mirrors, no bookcases and no closets. Lindy's personal space was her bed. She had hung her few keepsakes over two bedposts, and extra clothes were stored under her bed. Next door was a playroom for younger children. The population at most Chinese orphanages is entirely female. However, in Fushun, because of the number of children with physical and cognitive disabilities, both boys and girls filled the playrooms. There were few toys.

The orphanage is also home to a number of healthy older teens who grew up in different orphanages and came to live in Fushun to attend schools nearby. Lindy had suffered a serious neck injury from a fall and was not permitted to attend school. She proudly showed us her desk in another room. A tutor visits her once a week to help her with her studies. Lindy was not receiving any physical therapy, nor were the other children in the orphanage. I was informed that the children's parents were unable to afford to take care of them. The one-child policy makes it extremely difficult for parents to care for a second daughter, or a disabled child. Sons are preferred.

Lindy grew up in the orphanage and was now too old to be adopted. Chinese law does not allow for adoption after age fourteen. She has an aunt living in the area who was unable to care for her and was unwilling to release her for adoption at a younger age. Lindy has a slight chance to eventually attend the local university. However, it is more likely that she will live her life working at the orphanage as a nanny or working for low wages in one of the local factories.

A heart for Lebanon. Camille Melki was raised in Beirut and attended a Christian university in the United States. He became a leader of EQUIP, an international training ministry that provides resources for Christian leaders worldwide. In 2006, Camille, with his wife, Hoda, began a new ministry, Heart for Lebanon, as a response to the over-whelming needs created by the war.[12] A member of the ministry who was working among the Gypsies and the Bedouin tribal leaders heard that a planeload of young women was going to be transported to Arab Gulf countries to work as escorts and dancers in nightclubs. They would be stripped of their passports and become virtual slaves, isolated in foreign countries. Their parents, unable to support them, agreed, along with their tribal leaders, to send them to these countries with the assurance of jobs for their daughters. This ministry leader was able to persuade the parents and the tribal authorities not to send the youth abroad with the promise that Heart for Lebanon would provide jobs for these young women. The ministry moved their soap-making business to Beirut in order to expand it and provide jobs for these teens and women.

These small businesses are a necessary means of survival for women at risk of being sold into slavery. They offer financial independence, which offers empowerment and a life free from oppression and abuse. Sex trafficking is rampant not only in the Middle East but throughout Asia, Europe, the United States and most countries in the world.

Violence against women is systematic and part of the structural fabric of our cultures, politics, economic systems and traditions. Ashmita experienced familial shunning and rejection simply because she was born a female. Lindy, although loved by her nannies, was without a family, as are millions of females in China. The teenage girls in Lebanon prepared to depart for a life of sexual slavery because the girls' parents could not afford to care for them. The parents needed the income that they hoped would be sent to them. The girls would have been exploited in a horrific manner had it not been for a group of concerned Christians, supported by many churches scattered throughout the world, who entered into Christ's work among the poor and oppressed. These Christians shared the whole of the gospel. They proclaimed the freedom of faith in Christ

---

[12]Camille E. Melki, "Women and Church History" (lecture handout, Northeastern Seminary, Rochester, NY, February 13, 2012).

and provided opportunities for the marginalized to live lives of dignity. The widespread atrocities experienced by women and girls in India, China and the Middle East are a small part of a global phenomenon of violence against women and girls. A moral and ethical response from the Christian church is only a partial response. What is needed is a powerful, holistic and missional response rooted in a biblical theology of the cross because a theology of the cross does not separate proclamation of the gospel from the prophetic and active role of working to end injustice for millions of women and girls. The work of ending violence against women and girls begins with prayer. Prayer positions us to reflect theologically on the relationship of faith and mission and moves us toward the work of social justice.

A THEOLOGY OF THE CROSS

A theology of the cross, as described in chapter four, is helpful in providing a foundation for both the language and description of the work in ending violence, and it offers a cohesive model for effective intervention. This discussion prompts the question, so what? (as I've been asked by many an insightful graduate student). Does it matter what the theological basis of the work is as long as aid is given to victims? My answer is a resounding yes! When the ultimate reality of God is in right relationship to the penultimate realities of our social and political systems, then the demand to worship God and serve one's neighbor becomes the confessional mandate for the *whole* church. The ultimate reality of the cross of Christ is pivotal to this theological argument and becomes the point of departure for the entire church to respond. However, the American Christian church has often succumbed to two inadequate responses: either ignoring the problem altogether or compartmentalizing gendercide into a "women's issue." In turn, all social problems become minimized. These insufficient responses are eliminated when embracing a theological foundation of the cross of Christ. The incarnational mission of Jesus as proclaimed in Luke 4:18-19 *is* the mission of the church:

The Spirit of the Lord is upon me,
    because he has anointed me
        to bring good news to the poor.
He has sent me to proclaim release to the captives
    and recovery of sight to the blind,
        to let the oppressed go free,
to proclaim the year of the Lord's favor.

Without theological reflection, the Christian community is in danger of adopting an attitude and a position that are reactive, rather than thoughtfully responsive, to global and social problems. With a strong commitment to theological reflection, as understood through a perspective of the cross and its subsequent implications for our orientation and care for our neighbor, there are several possible outcomes for church response. The following are five reasons why the theological approach to the work of ending violence against women and girls should be grounded in prayer, reflection and a theology of the cross.

First, confessions of faith express our understanding of our God and of how we relate to God. This is the starting point for response. The church holds to its confessions of faith to remember who this God is that is worshiped and what the identity of believers is in relation to God and others. Without continued reflection and remembrance, the community is in danger of divorcing itself not only from the meaning of the gift of faith in Christ but from the meaning of the Christian way of life. Subsequently, other ideologies, political, social or philosophical, can easily be substituted for the gospel. Throughout Christian history, there have been times when the church has strayed from its roots in the confession of Christ. Prophets have risen in various locations and centuries to remind the church of the nature of the faithful God and its communal identity and mission. During the last century, Reinhold Niebuhr, Dorothy Day, Dietrich Bonhoeffer, Martin Luther King Jr., Mother Teresa and Oscar Romero have been but a few of those voices reminding the church of the gospel demand to be faithful to the God known through Word and sacrament, through proclamation *and* ministry.

Second, theological reflection offers an opportunity to engage in deeper discussions regarding the consequences of faith. Eberhard Bethge noted that Dietrich Bonhoeffer and members of the Confessing Church slowly began to realize through the increasing darkness of National Socialism that church attendance and the recitation of confession were not enough to care for the oppressed, and did nothing to stop Nazi atrocities.[13] Confessions and doctrine can be detached from the call to active response and mission. Recitations of confessions, as well as attendance at liturgies and church functions, do not ensure an understanding of the penultimate realities of social, political and religious problems. There are painful reminders of this detached confessionalism and its subsequent lack of response to injustice in our history, marked by racism, oppression of women and economic injustices inflicted on the poor, to name a few. Our history also contains hopeful reminders that the church can join the confession of the faith with active response. Dorothy Day's challenge to the church to care for the poor, Desmond Tutu's call to end apartheid and the activism of Archbishop Romero to aid the poor in El Salvador are only a few examples of leaders who understood that theological reflection on the meaning of confession and our identity in Christ must lead to resistance to unjust systems and social activism.

Third, a theological foundation of the cross offers an orientation centered on an incarnational Christ as the pivotal point in the church's care for the other. The ultimate gift of salvation through the cross of Christ is connected in a dialectical relationship to the response of faith, that is, love of neighbor. Theological reflection, by the whole Christian community, therefore, demands a unified response. All members of the church community are required to engage in both proclamation of the gospel and service to neighbor. The nature of this service is often limited to individual philanthropy. However, the Scriptures are clear that care

---

[13]Eberhard Bethge, *Friendship and Resistance: Essays on Dietrich Bonhoeffer* (Grand Rapids: Eerdmans, 1995), p. 24. See further discussion on the relationship of confession and resistance in chapter four, "The Cross and the Promise: God for Us."

for our neighbors includes prophetic calls to end injustice; resistance to religious, social and political systems of oppression; and identification with the poor and marginalized in society. Obedience to the demand to care for the oppressed and the suffering is required of all who call themselves Christian. This profound and clear command is given by Jesus. The Sermon on the Mount is not merely a dutiful prescription of how to live but rather a description of the Christian life. Therefore, to abide in the confession and spirituality of Christian faith is to abide in the essential mission of Christ.

This call to discipleship is seemingly obvious. Yet, calls to care for the poor and oppressed and to denounce unjust systems that maintain material and physical deprivation are often met by resistance by faithful Christians. Philanthropy and charity are often applauded and encouraged while the call for changes in systems that support injustice is met with suspicion and division within the Christian community. Care for our neighbor involves individual care, but it also includes a challenge to institutions that promote the subjugation of one gender over another, racial discrimination and economic injustice. This challenge divides Christian communities because it also challenges Christians' attachments to materialism, consumerism and social roles that bring comfort and security. However, deeper reflections by the church community on the meaning of a theology of the cross can create a foundation that promotes all of life. Global violence against women and girls can be greatly reduced by a more unified response of action by the whole of the Christian community. An adoption of what Cardinal Bernardin termed "a consistent ethic of life"[14] reflects a more faithful response to the gospel rather than an individualistic and pietistic ethic founded on political ideologies. Deep reflection on a theology of the cross can lead to a more unified Christian response.

Fourth, theological reflection on the meaning of our confession of

---

[14]Joseph Bernardin, "A Consistent Ethic of Life: An American-Catholic Dialogue" (Gannon Lecture, Fordham University, December 6, 1983), www.hnp.org/publications/hnpfocus/BConsistent Ethic1983.pdf.

Christ leads to a deeper understanding of spirituality and its relationship to justice. There exists not only in the church, but also within academia, a compartmentalization between theology, spiritual formation and ethics. This is a modern dilemma. Historically, the church lived out its identity within a worshiping community that integrated worship with its care for the poor and its call to live out justice in society.[15] Community prayer practices in many churches point to this incarnational understanding of connection between confession, worship and care for the poor. At the conclusion of some liturgies, the cross is carried down the aisle, the community then turns to follow the cross, and ultimately they face the back of the church, symbolizing the whole community's commitment to the "liturgy after the liturgy." The last words heard before dismissal are "go and serve the poor." Simple, and yet this employs powerful physical and spiritual movement and language that symbolize and describe a radical life of faith. The worship of God within church walls extends to worshiping God through care and love to the community's neighbors. Since ancient times, this radical act of hospitality has always been integrated into the very heart and life of the church.

Both Dorothy Day and Dietrich Bonhoeffer embraced the cost of living out their confessions of faith concretely and completely. Dorothy Day faced support when carrying out the tasks of feeding and housing the poor, but great resistance within the same community of faith when she confronted the roots of political, social and religious systems of injustice. Recovering the Christian tradition of extending hospitality to the "stranger," so central to Christian spirituality and ethics, includes responding to both the individual stranger we may encounter in our local communities and those in need far from our homes. Knowledge of the plight of those exposed to global violence and poverty is not enough. The church must be engaged in care for abused women and children that live in both our local and global communities. Historically,

---

[15]See Carter Lindberg's description of the integration of church practice, liturgy and poor relief in *Beyond Charity: Reformation Initiatives for the Poor* (Minneapolis: Augsburg Fortress, 1993), pp. 163-69.

Christian spirituality and ethics were concerned with the care of the neighbor everywhere and the promotion of just institutions. The prophetic voice of the church is deeply rooted in the biblical mandate to care for the poor and denounce social, religious and political systems that support injustice. Dietrich Bonhoeffer equated life in Christ with identification with the victims of violence and oppression because he maintained that the "other" is Christ in the world. This strong incarnational life in Christ is the mark of authentic Christianity.

Theological reflection on this powerful dialectic of faith and ethics collapses false categories of theology, spiritual formation and ethics. An emphasis on spiritual disciplines as acts of piety is an anemic spirituality in a world where unjust systems support widespread poverty and violence. A spirituality that embraces hospitality extending to others outside of our own faith communities is a more faithful spirituality reflective of the gospel. Theological reflections on the cross can lead the church to a humility that opens the community to the needs of women and girls who have been battered and abused everywhere. All are created in the image of God. The rights and dignity of women and girls are bestowed by the creator God, and no one can rightfully rob them of their rights and dignity. Those that violate these rights, and collude by their silence and lack of action, commit grievous sins. The reality of the incarnation has meaning in shaping a faithful response to aid those who are oppressed and suffering.

Some years ago I spoke at a conference attended by college students in Boston. The topic was a faith response to domestic violence. During a morning break, a college student approached me with a stunned look on her face. She exclaimed, "I never knew that women were treated this way in the world. I've never heard this in church. And now that I know, I can *never not* know!" Implied in her exclamation was, "I now have to do something!" Obedience is demanded by the Christ who taught that feeding the poor, visiting the sick and caring for others was in essence caring for the One who came in poverty and in hiddenness. Evident in the incarnation and the cross is the paradox of both the revelation of

God and the hiddenness of God. Through the eyes of faith the church perceives and embraces the power of God made evident in weakness and worldly lowliness (1 Cor 1:18-31). The hiddenness of Christ in the cross continues to be present in those whose lives are hidden in poverty and subjugation. A faithful response to the gospel extends beyond pietistic, individual acts of charity. Committed acts of resistance by a unified church against political and social systems that continue to support violence against women and girls would characterize a church living out its confession of faith.

Fifth, our confession of faith leads to a deeper reflection on our language. How the church identifies global and social problems shapes its response. Theological language, rather than psychological language, is helpful in identifying violence against women and girls as sin, not merely a psychological or sociological problem. Not only is theological language important because it is the most accurate language to use, but it points the church in the right direction for response. Selective abortion of girls, genital mutilation, stoning, human trafficking, rape as a tool of war, sexual abuse, domestic violence in the home and other atrocities are human rights issues *and* they are sin. The church's proclamation of the gospel offers the hope of Christ for salvation and condemns all sin that violates the integrity and dignity of the human person. When the church defines these acts as sin, then it is compelled to condemn these acts, aid victims and work to overthrow systems that support its continuation. Violence against women and girls involves not only individual acts of violence. It involves and is supported by institutional and structural systems that enable the violence to continue unabated.

Theological language gives shape to a corporate church response by identifying violence against women and girls as sin and, subsequently, denouncing it as sin. This sin is a confessional issue because it violates the integrity of human beings, in this case because of their gender. Gendercide is a form of idolatry and goes beyond the need to identify it as a moral issue alone. The starting point for identifying violence against women and girls as a confessional issue and the necessary church response is the gospel. For the church, the use of the language of the gospel provides the orientation for addressing this critical issue. Bonhoeffer understood better than anyone in the twentieth century how critical it was for the church to clearly define the crisis in his own time, and he understood that the beginning of all activity begins with God.

> The kind of thinking that starts out from human problems and then looks for solutions from that vantage point, has to be overcome—it is unbiblical. The way of Jesus Christ, and thus the way of all Christian thought, is not the way from the world to God but from God to the world. This means that the essence of the gospel does not consist in solving worldly problems, and also that this cannot be the essential task of the church. However, it does not follow from this that the church would have no task in this regard. *But we will not recognize its legitimate task unless we first find the correct starting point.*[16]

The use of theological language to identify violence against women and girls from "the right point of departure" is helpful in framing a holistic, unified and powerfully effective response for the Christian church.

A theological approach to ending violence against women and girls reminds the church that the worship of our God must involve care for the poor, peacemaking and creating justice because theology is the proclamation of the God who cares for the oppressed and marginalized. Mission begins and ends in prayer and confession. It is always, for all time, the call of the Christian church. Therefore, our social activism is rooted in the proclamation of the suffering, hidden Christ of the cross, the Word of God. Theology shapes ecclesiology and mission. How intentional are our churches in doing the work of theological reflection? A theology of the cross is our lens for seeing more clearly the call God has for our lives and on our churches.

I propose that the Christian church revisit Martin Luther's theology of the cross and Dietrich Bonhoeffer's twentieth-century interpretation

---

[16]Dietrich Bonhoeffer, *Ethics,* trans. Reinhard Krauss, Charles C. West and Douglas W. Stott, and ed. Clifford J. Green, vol. 6 of *Dietrich Bonhoeffer Works—English Edition* (Minneapolis: Fortress, 2005), p. 356, emphasis added.

of that theology within the context of Nazi racism and church identity. This book offers a more radical, nuanced interpretation of a theology of the cross for the twenty-first century, one that emphasizes the encounter of the living Christ within our identification with and relationship to the poor, suffering and oppressed. Hospitality is radicalized and globalized. Therefore, care for the "other" includes the neighbor who is "farthest." However, before exploring the meaning and important themes of this theology, it is critical to understand more deeply the atrocities and widespread prevalence of global violence against women and girls.

2

THE NUMBERS AND THE STORIES

The Extent of the Violence

VIOLENCE AGAINST WOMEN is a serious social, spiritual, health and legal problem in the United States. However, it is only one facet of a complex and tangled web of atrocities committed against women and girls globally. The term *gendercide* is the best descriptor of this global problem, which impacts women, girls, families and whole societies. Different governmental and private agencies publish varying statistics, but all the numbers are staggering and difficult to absorb and comprehend. Nevertheless, it is important to comprehend the extent and nature of the problem and its complexity in order to understand it as a confessional issue as well as a moral and ethical issue.

Violence against women and girls is defined by the World Health Organization as "any act of gender-based violence that results in physical, sexual, or psychological harm or suffering to women, including threats of such acts, coercion, or arbitrary deprivations of liberty, whether occurring in public or private life."[1] The violence perpetrated against women and girls occurs in many different settings, including in the home, within the community and during armed conflict. It takes the forms of sexual assault, female genital mutilation (FGM), sex trafficking, domestic violence, forced abortions, infanticide of girl babies, honor killings, rape as a weapon of war, and exploitation of women and girls in labor for profit. Statistics reveal only a small part of the story of

---

[1]World Health Organization, *Violence Against Women: Fact Sheet No. 239*, rev. ed. (Geneva: WHO, 2009).

women and girls. Each survivor of violence has her own story of how acts of violation shattered her life and the life of her family. Pain and shame have ripped apart both the bodies and psyches of these women and girls along with their families and communities. However, the numbers are also part of this story for they reveal the underlying causes of violence, including domination, misogyny and objectification of females. They also point to the grave sin of gendercide, which needs to be addressed by the *whole* of the church as a confessional issue rather than as a moral and legal issue, which only marginalizes the problem.

The systemic causes of violence against women and girls have social, religious and cultural roots. Historical acceptance of the domination and objectification of females is a reality within every global culture and history. The predominant expression of violence against women in the United States takes the form of domestic violence and sexual assault. More women and girls are injured by a family member or intimate than by a stranger. The word *domestic* describes the most frequent location of violence; however, it tends to minimize the seriousness of the violence. Women and girls in the United States are not exposed to female genital mutilation, rape used as a weapon of war, acid throwing, female infanticide and other horrific injustices. Nevertheless, the stories of torture, rape, beatings and other forms of violence remain a national tragedy and part of our social fabric. Although all statistics and expressions of violence against women and girls are mind numbing and heart wrenching to hear and read about, it is vital that Christians attempt to absorb the complexity and widespread characteristics of this problem. The sheer numbers of victims and survivors of violence are convincing enough for the church to begin to identify this violence as global gendercide. This is a genocide of women and girls that is more difficult to grasp given that it is a global rather than a local problem. However, the sheer numbers alone reflect the same definitions we have had of other genocides in modern times.

THE UNITED STATES

There have been numerous studies and research that conclude that violence against women in the United States is a major health and social problem. Statistics vary slightly from one source to another. However, statistics have been kept by governments, women's organizations and other researchers for the past thirty to forty years and have given us a consistent picture of the problem. An estimated 1.3 million women are victims of physical assault by an intimate partner each year. Of all victims of violence 85 to 95 percent are women and girls. We know that females between the ages of twenty and twenty-four years are at the greatest risk of nonfatal intimate partner violence. These numbers reflect the reported cases of violence to the police. Most incidents never get reported.[2] Approximately one-quarter of physical assaults, one-fifth of all rapes and one-half of all stalking perpetrated against females by intimate partners are reported to authorities.[3]

The statistics are just that, statistics that tell us the scope of the problem. More telling are the stories of women in our local communities and local churches. These women and girls are our neighbors, attend local school meetings, work at the same jobs and sit next us in the pews on Sunday. The visibility of this problem has increased in recent years as a result of media coverage, special domestic-violence-awareness and sexual-assault-designated months, and memorials to remember the victims. There has been a proliferation of literature on the subject during the last thirty-five years, and pressure from grassroots women's organizations has helped to raise awareness and change laws to protect the rights of victims. However, the narratives told by survivors of violence tell a more layered story. Their stories reveal a continued stubbornness on the part of many institutions to create a no-tolerance milieu that would make it very difficult for violence to be tolerated in our churches, families and society. During more than

---

[2]These statistics were gathered from the National Coalition Against Domestic Violence website: www .ncadv.org/files/DomesticViolenceFactSheet(National).pdf. They are a summary of various studies. See also US Bureau of Justice website: www.bjs.gov/content/pub/pdf/fvs.pdf.

[3]Patricia Tjaden and Nancy Thoennes, *Extent, Nature and Consequences of Intimate Partner Violence: Findings from the National Violence Against Women Survey* (Washington, DC: US Department of Justice, Office of Justice Programs, National Institute of Justice, 2000), www.ncjrs.gov/pdffiles1/ nij/181867.pdf, p. iii.

twenty-five years of counseling abused women and teens in various settings, including shelters, private counseling, church groups, and in local
district and family courts, I have been a witness to the response of
church leaders and laity, legal authorities, child welfare advocates and
many others who offer support and help to survivors. I have also witnessed responses rooted in fear and ignorance that continue to per-
petuate the stereotypes and that also continue the oppression experienced by many victims. The following are a few of these stories. (All
names and identifying features have been changed.)

Mary Ann. Mary Ann had been abused for over twenty years in her
marriage, during which time she had never sought a safe shelter or legal
protection. Finally, she came to the shelter alone and sought out any
quiet space she could while avoiding conversation. After a few days she
began to tell her story. She described a husband who isolated her from
her immediate family members and others in her community. She was
regularly beaten when she failed to perform a household chore or task
in the way that her husband demanded. She described violence that
consisted of both verbal and physical abuse. There was ongoing verbal
name calling and almost daily hitting, shaking, slapping, shoving and
throwing up against walls. Her isolation was so complete that she cried
as she sat at the kitchen table drinking coffee with the other women
residing at the shelter. Up until this time she had shown no emotion
while reporting the horrible violence that she had experienced. When
asked why she was crying now, she responded that it was the first time
in twenty years she had had a cup of coffee with other women. She also
reported that she had never sought shelter or help from anyone in the
community before because she knew he would eventually find her and
kill her. However, this last incident was so violent she decided he was
going to kill her if she stayed. Therefore, she was willing to take a chance
to run away and hide out at the shelter.

Slowly over time Mary Ann was able to describe the last incident
that brought her to the shelter. She stood in the driveway while her
husband towered over her screaming obscenities. He grabbed her by

the throat and pushed her up against the door of the garage. She passed out, but as she began to return to consciousness she saw his car coming toward her. He pinned her against the garage door and she passed out again. She regained consciousness in the hospital. Fortunately, a neighbor witnessed what was happening and called the police. Mary Ann finally realized, while recuperating in the hospital, that to return home was a death sentence. She called the shelter from the hospital and found safety and, for the first time, supportive friends and advocates. Mary Ann never returned home. Through months of supportive counseling she began to regain her self-confidence and live independently.

Linda. Unlike Mary Ann, Linda had sought support from different agencies and institutions in her community before coming to the shelter. Linda had been repeatedly raped by her husband and gang raped by a few of his friends. The child welfare advocate did not believe her story because it was too "unbelievable," and her pastor thought she should work harder at the marriage. One afternoon as she related the remarks of the social worker and her pastor she broke down in tears. This lack of affirmation, particularly from her pastor, caused her to question the seriousness of her situation, and she felt victimized by the representatives of her church community.

After several sessions of counseling, Linda slowly learned that she had self-worth and that she truly did have the power to create boundaries between herself and those who infringe upon her dignity. She also learned that marriage was not a license to sexually abuse and rape her and that her safety and life were important to God. She found a church that supported her healing. The response of her pastor was wrong, but he had learned through his own religious education that marriage was the wife's responsibility and that it was her duty to fix any problems. This pastor represented the thinking of many pastors that I have worked with over the years. There was, and continues to be, in many churches this continued gap between theology, on the one hand, and social justice and practice, on the other. Idolatry takes on many forms, including the belief that abuse against women for the sake of keeping marriages together is tolerable.

Monique. Monique entered counseling when she was twenty-two years old. She had attended a vigil for sexual assault victims at her Christian college and was unexpectedly surprised by memories that surfaced immediately following that event. She felt anxious, unable to focus on her work and haunted by memories of an event that happened when she was a young girl. Over several sessions she slowly revealed an incident that she had worked fifteen years to forget. She had been brutally raped by a distant family member. The attack was sudden and violent in every sense. As a young girl she was terrified, physically hurt and shamed. After the attack, Monique sat alone in her room feeling fear and confusion.

Monique found she could no longer forget the assault, as it became a daily obsession, and nightmares disturbed her sleep. She was finding it difficult to concentrate. She cried frequently and was beginning to experience panic attacks. Throughout her teen years she had experienced depressions and had suicidal ideation, which temporarily eased the psychic and emotional pain. She was very active in her church, led a large teen group and was herself a part of a young adults group. She had never spoken to former counselors or church leaders about this event that was so horrific. She had psychologically buried it and never spoke of it throughout her childhood. For years she carried those feelings of fear and confusion with her. She related how she had always felt like an outsider in the teen groups she attended. Her church leaders emphasized the importance of abstinence and the importance of the girls maintaining their virginity. She sadly described how ashamed she felt as a result of believing that she was not a virgin and, subsequently, that she had sinned.

What Monique described is indicative of many church teen groups. With the best of intentions, they teach the sacredness of sexuality but fail to acknowledge that approximately 25 percent of the girls in their churches have already been sexually assaulted or have suffered an assault attempt. Monique sat for years in church believing that she was the only girl that had experienced sexual assault. She later found that she was not alone. As she began to work through her own grief and pain, she also became more open to talking to her friends and teen group, of which she was a leader, about violence against women and girls. It didn't take long to discover that others in her church had also experienced abuse in some form. Churches that are open to providing safe havens and resources for girls and women to talk about their stories of victimization and survival find that there are many survivors that sit in the pews each Sunday feeling just like Monique, ashamed and alone. Education, support and a no-tolerance attitude toward abusive behavior can be shaped by our churches by practicing a theology centered on Christ who is present in the reality of suffering.

These are only a few stories among hundreds I have heard over the years in many community settings and from women and teens of various ethnic, socioeconomic and religious backgrounds. The stories differ in details, but the abusive behaviors have a common theme of acts of objectification and domination. The hitting, punching, choking, isolation, name calling, sexual assault, rape and other violent acts are rooted in the perpetrator's desire for power and control and domination. However, the problems extend beyond one individual's behavior toward another. There are systemic causes of violence against women and girls rooted in religious traditions, cultural norms and history. The existence of safe shelters, counseling, restraining-order laws and guidelines, mandatory arrest procedures, and public-awareness campaigns emerged in the recent history of the United States. These are welcome changes for thousands of battered women and their families. Marge, a seventy-five-year-old victim of abuse, reported that she had survived over fifty years in an abusive marriage and that until recently had nowhere to go. "There were no shelters, no way to get out safely all these years. I never thought that I could completely escape. How nice these women today have someplace to go!" Many churches are stepping up and realizing that inaction and silence are forms of collusion and are indeed a sinful response to a critical problem.

A confession of one's faith in Christ must lead to action and resistance to cultural norms that still support the economic inequalities of women and men[4] and the objectification of women. Domestic violence and sexual assault continue to be a critical problem in the United States, and the foundation of violence still needs to be challenged in every arena, including the Christian church. Globally, the incidence and ferocity of the problem appear more overwhelming than in the United States because of a lack of legal protections. From China to Africa, and throughout every country, violence against women and girls is so pervasive that it deserves to be compared to other modern genocides. Whether the location is somewhere in the United States, Africa, Asia, South America or any other corner of the world, the devastation and effects of violence that tear through women's and girls' lives can never be overstated. Nevertheless, there is hope in every dark corner, and there is much work that a united Christian church can do if founded on the cross of a Savior who is always *for* life.

THE GLOBAL PROBLEM OF GENDERCIDE

China. One of the most devastating catastrophes to happen in our modern era is the human toll of the one-child policy in China. While undergoing a massive famine that killed thirty million people between 1958 and 1961,[5] Mao Zedong perpetuated the policy of building a strong China through the continued practice of rejecting Western ideas of birth control. However, in the early 1970s, the government became convinced that economic growth and increased power came not from an increase in population but from putting into place a policy that would ultimately lead to infanticide, forced abortions and the abandonment of millions of baby girls in China. A decrease in population, government leaders argued, would lead to greater stability in China and increased success in becoming powerful among emerging nations.

---

[4]According to the 2010 census, American women make only 80 percent of men's earnings in similar jobs. See http://blogs.census.gov/2010/09/23/income-vs-earnings.

[5]Karin Evans, *The Lost Daughters of China* (New York: Penguin Putnam, 2000), p. 96.

The 1980 marriage law and 1982 constitution set basic policy for requiring couples to limit themselves to one child.[6] In fact, the goal was that couples would have 1.6 children when exceptions to the policy were taken into account.[7] In effect it took away all rights of couples in the area of conceiving and bearing children. Women needed permission to conceive and give birth. A woman needed to complete official paperwork in order to go to the hospital to give birth. There were benefits to obeying the edict. A couple would receive preferential treatment in securing housing and medical care. There were serious consequences for couples not keeping to the requirements by law. They could be fined, be taxed, lose their jobs and be put in jail. Children born outside of the birth plan and without government approval were denied the resident registration card that needed to secure health benefits and eventually a job.[8]

The long arm of the Chinese state reached into every household. Women who became pregnant without permission were confronted and, if officials decided it was necessary, marched to abortion clinics. Once a child was born, a woman was required to have an IUD inserted and periodically checked. After the birth of a second child, either husband or wife was to be sterilized. Forced sterilizations, mandatory insertions of metal IUDs—which could be monitored by X rays to make sure they remained in place—became commonplace assaults on the women of China, as did forced abortions, even at full term. . . . Officials of the Women's Federation of the Communist Party kept track of women's monthly cycles, and listed those to be sterilized and those required to have IUDs inserted.[9]

---

[6]See the Human Rights in China website, www.hrichina.org, for a detailed history and description of the one-child policy in China.

[7]Evans, *Lost Daughters,* p. 98.

[8]See www.christusrex.org/www1/sdc/hr_facts.html#Woman for information on women and children compiled in a fact sheet that was prepared by the Robert F. Kennedy Memorial Center for Human Rights. It is based on information provided by Amnesty International-USA, the Committee to Protect Journalists, the Francois-Xavier Bagnoud Center for Health and Human Rights, Human Rights in China, the International Campaign for Tibet, the Puebla Institute and the RFK Memorial Center for Human Rights.

[9]Evans, *Lost Daughters,* p. 100.

The burden of complying fell primarily on women since they were the ones that were usually sterilized. They went through the trauma of forced abortions even into the ninth month. The violation of their bodies with the insertion of IUDs and tracking of their cycles, including periodic checks to insure that the IUD was in place, constituted institutionalized rape. The violation was both physical and emotional and took a toll on the mental and physical health of millions of women.

During the campaigns of 1983 and 1991, thirty million women were forcibly sterilized.[10] In addition to the dehumanization of women through forced sterilizations and abortions, it is estimated that millions of baby girls have been killed and abandoned in China. In 1990, the renowned Indian economist Amartya Sen put the number of Asian females missing, aborted, killed, neglected or put to death at one hundred million. Approximately fifty million of those are females that would be alive today in China had it not been for the preference for males and the subsequent atrocities. The one-child policy varies from one rural area to another and one city to another. In some places women are allowed to have more than one child if the second child is a boy. Abandoned girls are often second or later children born to a woman with one daughter and hoping for a son.

Chinese mothers find themselves in the untenable circumstance of being forced to abandon their daughters while at the same time facing criminal charges if they are caught giving up their children. Their choices are so limited that the result is tens of thousands of baby girls being abandoned in marketplaces or other places where mothers hope they will be quickly found and brought to an orphanage. This means that they will never see their children again or learn if their hope for foreign adoption and better lives for their daughters is ever realized. Not all abandoned babies are girls, though approximately 95 percent of the babies in orphanages in China are girls. The one-child policy has also contributed to the practice of prenatal sex identification resulting in the abortion of female fetuses. Although the government has outlawed the

[10]Ibid., p. 106.

use of ultrasound machines for this purpose, physicians continue the practice, especially in rural areas. An April 2009 study by the *British Medical Journal (BMJ)* found that China still has 32 million more boys than girls under the age of twenty.[11] Therefore, while the average worldwide ratio of male to female newborns is 105 to 100, statistics show that the ratio in the People's Republic of China (PRC) in 2000–2004 is 124 males to 100 females born. It is estimated that in some provinces the number is even higher, reaching 130 males to 100 females.

The psychological impact on women forced to give up or abort their daughters is devastating. Female suicide rates in China are among the highest in the world. Suicide is the most common form of death among Chinese rural women ages fifteen to thirty-four.[12] The author Xinran Xue has collected personal narratives describing the devastating impact of the one-child policy in China. She described seeing a newborn baby girl grabbed from her mother after childbirth and thrown head first into a chamber pot. She heard this newborn move within the pot. Xinran Xue jumped out of her chair to rescue the baby. Family members restrained her, and she was told it was too late. The baby was dead. Years later she met the baby's mother again, and the mother reported that she was forced to give up two more daughters to foreigners. She asked Xinran whether foreigners know the right way to hold a baby.[13]

Violence against women and girls extends to spousal abuse. According to some researchers, spousal abuse is far too common in China and, in many parts of the country, still socially acceptable. However, comprehensive statistics about the extent of domestic violence are not available or have not been made public. The official All-China Women's Federation (ACWF) has been studying this problem and has found that few battered women have the opportunity to escape abuse because

---

[11]Wei Xing Zhu, Li Lu and Therese Hesketh, "China's Excess Males, Sex Selective Abortion, and One Child Policy: Analysis of Data from 2005 National Intercensus Survey," *BMJ* 338, no. 7700 (April 18, 2009): 920-23.

[12]Xinran Xue, "Gendercide: The Worldwide War on Baby Girls," *Economist*, March 4, 2010, www .economist.com/node/15636231.

[13]Xinran Xue, *Message from an Unknown Chinese Mother: Stories of Loss and Love*, trans. Nicky Harman (New York: Simon and Schuster, 2010).

shelters and other resources are not available. Women are under considerable social pressure to keep families together regardless of the circumstances. Legal action is not taken against batterers unless the victim initiates it, and if she withdraws her testimony, the proceedings are ended.

Trafficking and the sale of women as brides or into prostitution are serious problems in certain parts of China, and Chinese women have been sold into brothels in Southeast Asia. The PRC government has enacted various laws to combat the sale of women, but the statistics released by the government do not reliably indicate the scale of the problem. Chinese officials stated that there were fifteen thousand cases of kidnapping and trafficking in women and children in 1993. Yet according to one estimate, ten thousand women were abducted and sold in 1992 in Sichuan Province alone. Until recently, the authorities have not prosecuted men who purchase women as wives. Therefore, the trade has continued unabated. Official action to rescue victims of trafficking is generally initiated only if a complaint is made by the woman or her family. Local officials often turn a blind eye, even formally registering marriages into which the woman has been sold. The PRC ratified the Convention on the Elimination of All Forms of Discrimination Against Women in 1980 and enacted the Law on the Protection of Women's Rights and Interests in 1992. However, open discrimination against women and girls in China continues unabated.

Economic inequality continues to exist in a country where per capita income is approximately $1900 in urban areas and $600 in rural areas.[14] According to China's government surveys, women's salaries have been found to average 77 percent of men's, and most women employed in industry work in low-skill and low-paying jobs. The proportion of women to men declines at each educational tier, with women constituting some 25 percent of undergraduates in universities. Institutions of higher education that have a large proportion of female applicants, such

---

[14]"Children Go Home as China Cracks Trafficking Ring," *Reuters-Africa*, January 3, 2008, adapted by Humantrafficking.org, www.humantrafficking.org/updates/827.

as foreign-language institutes, have been known to require higher entrance-exam grades from women. During two recent visits to China, it was evident to me that women were the face of low-paying jobs in factories, hotel services and orphanages. All decision-making positions were held by men. As China's economy continues to grow, more opportunities are opening for women, but social and economic inequality continues to oppress millions of Chinese women and girls.

Human trafficking. The causes of human trafficking are complex. Trafficking of persons is part of a global network that is lucrative for the sellers, creates cheap labor for abusive and sexual predators and is devastating for the victims. Because of dire poverty and the attraction of money offered to parents for their daughters with the understanding that a better life awaits the girls, the supply of predominantly female victims never dwindles. Young women are offered jobs overseas with the promise of adequate income for a better life. These are not the only underlying causes of trafficking, but poverty, coupled with the objectification and denigration of females, fuels a trade that has fingers in most countries around the world.

The numbers of victims vary from one source to another; nevertheless, the estimate of 800,000 to 2 million offers a glimpse into a horrific problem that is difficult to determine. Men, women and children are targeted by traffickers, but the US Department of State reports that approximately 80 percent are women and girls and 50 percent of that number are minors. The numbers are so alarming that it is widely acknowledged as fact that human slavery in the twentieth and twenty-first century is larger than the slave trade during the sixteenth and seventeenth centuries. Traffickers often pose as agents of legitimate employment agencies and promise hopeful futures to the children of poor parents. Parents eager to secure a better life for their children trade them for money that will help feed and shelter their other children. Daughters often find themselves employed not in good jobs as promised but rather as sex slaves in brothels, as workers in filthy sweatshops or as house slaves for wealthy buyers. Both boys and girls can find themselves working long hours seven days a week for little or no money and no way out. Trafficking continues to be driven by the global demand for cheap, illegal and vulnerable labor.

Traffickers take advantage of natural disasters to kidnap children who have been abruptly orphaned. In the aftermath of the December 26, 2004, tsunami in the Indian Ocean, there were reports of rape, sexual abuse and trafficking in Sri Lanka and other countries devastated by the tsunami. Thousands of children were made vulnerable by natural disaster—and by those criminals seeking profit. As a result, governments and NGOs make the prevention of human trafficking an integral component of disaster relief efforts.[15] After the shocking earthquake that took place in Haiti in 2010, incidents of sexual assaults, rapes and attempts to kidnap children were reported to various news and relief organizations. Traffickers target the most vulnerable and seek to provide the "goods" to buyers that will pay the most. This means women and girls are especially vulnerable because of their gender and marketability. The dehumanization and objectification of women and girls are part of the criminal and sinful world of gendercide.

Sex tourism and child pornography are global industries fueled by new technologies, including the Internet, which makes pornography more accessible to those demanding cheap and secret transactions. Since 2000 there has been an increase in the prosecution of child sex tourism (CST) offenses. At least thirty-two countries have extraterritorial laws that allow the prosecution of their citizens' CST crimes committed abroad. In response to the problem of CST, many governments, NGOs and the tourism industry have begun to address the issue. The World Tourism Organization (WTO) established a task force to combat CST. The WTO; the NGO End Child Prostitution, Child Pornography and Trafficking of Children for Sexual Purposes; and Nordic tour operators created a global Code of Conduct for the Protection of Children from

---

[15]US Department of State, Office to Monitor and Combat Trafficking in Persons, *Trafficking in Persons Report* (June 3, 2005), www.state.gov/g/tip/rls/tiprpt/2005/46606.htm. See for a complete government report on the extent of global human trafficking.

Sexual Exploitation in Travel and Tourism in 1999.[16] In 2003, the United States passed the Prosecutorial Remedies and Other Tools to End the Exploitation of Children Today (PROTECT) Act and The Trafficking Victims Protection Reauthorization Act in order to strengthen its ability to combat CST. Together these laws increase penalties to a maximum of thirty years in prison for engaging in CST. The Department of Homeland Security has also developed the Operation Predator initiative to fight child exploitation.[17] Christian organizations such as Catholic Relief Services, Catholic Migration Commission, International Justice Mission (IJM) and World Vision are partnering with government agencies and NGOs to educate and provide services to victims of trafficking.

Sexual violence. Among the most disturbing of gender-related atrocities is female genital mutilation (FGM). It involves the removal of sensitive female genital organs. This is done through crude surgery, usually performed by women in rural areas. The traditional practice takes place throughout parts of Africa, Asia, the Middle East, Latin America and Australia. FGM is performed as part of a rite-of-passage ceremony, usually on defenseless females entering puberty. The practice is an attempt to control a girl's sexuality and ensure her virginity before marriage. In some areas the belief is that the clitoris is a male characteristic of the woman and needs to be removed in order for her to be "clean" and maintain her femininity. FGM is usually performed by an "excisor," who depends on this employment for her livelihood. The conditions are often unhygienic, and the crude instruments can leave long-lasting scarring and damage to the girls' genital organs. A kitchen knife, a razor blade or a piece of glass is the usual tool of the trade. The operation takes approximately ten to twenty minutes without anesthetic. The child is held down by three or four women, and the wound may be treated with cow dung, local herbs or butter.[18]

---

[16]See www.thecode.org.

[17]US Department of State, *Trafficking in Persons Report*, pp. 19-20.

[18]Office of the High Commissioner for Human Rights, *Harmful Traditional Practices Affecting the Health of Women and Children: Fact Sheet No. 23* (Geneva: Office of the High Commissioner for Human Rights, 2004), p. 5.

The pain experienced by young girls physically forced to undergo this procedure is horrific, and the damaging effects can be lasting. Physical complications can occur during FGM, including heavy loss of blood, infections, infertility caused by infection, obstructed labor and psychological distress caused by trauma. If the remaining vaginal opening is too small, menstrual blood that is unable to pass may cause further infection to other organs and may later prevent pregnancy. Death is also a danger because of loss of blood, infection or severe scarring that ruptures during childbirth.[19] An estimated 100 to 140 million girls and women worldwide are currently living with the consequences of FGM. The greatest numbers of affected girls are in Africa with an estimated 92 million ages ten and above having undergone the procedure.[20]

Another violation of girls' dignity in many countries is early marriage. The practice of offering girls for marriage at the age of eleven through fourteen is prevalent in parts of Asia and Africa, with the expectation that these girls will produce children soon after marriage. Marriage at such an early age increases the likelihood that girls will still be virgins at the age they marry and therefore command a higher dowry. Early marriage often inflicts psychological and physical trauma to children. Young brides have to abruptly leave their families of origin at a young age and live with husbands that are invariably much older. They are expected to engage in sexual activity and are frequently not physically developed enough for intercourse. Many of these girls come from communities where daughters experience neglect and discrimination and parents have a strong preference for sons. Many girls are promised as young as a few months old to the highest bidder.[21] In areas of South Asia, the status of girls is so low that payment of the dowry is given to the husband from the family of the girls. Tragically, when the dowry is not paid, a number of dowry crimes can occur, including mental and physical torture, starvation, rape and the burning alive of women by

---

[19]Ibid.
[20]World Health Organization, *Female Genital Mutilation: Fact Sheet No. 241* (Geneva: WHO, 2010).
[21]Office of the High Commissioner, *Harmful Traditional Practices*, p. 11.

their husbands. Many girls suffer disfigurement from acid thrown on their faces as punishment for refusing to marry or attempting to leave a prearranged marriage.

The rape of women and girls in war-torn areas is another atrocity of which the church is increasingly becoming aware. Rape is certainly not a modern tool of war. It is one of the oldest weapons of war. But until very recently rape was considered part of the collateral damage of war. It is now defined as a war crime. During war an estimated 20,000 rapes were committed in Bosnia, as well as 64,000 rapes in Sierra Leone and 500,000 rapes in Rwanda. In these three arenas alone there have been only forty-one convictions![22] However, in 1998, the International Criminal Tribunal for Rwanda declared rape an act of genocide, and in 2008 the United Nations Security Council adopted a resolution recognizing rape as a "tactic of war that is a crime against humanity." In August 2009 Secretary of State Hillary Clinton protested sexual violence during a visit to eastern Congo where an estimated 200,000 people have been abused in war. Two-thirds of the 16,000 sexual crimes were committed against girls and children.[23] An extensive study commissioned by Oxfam and conducted by Harvard Humanitarian Initiative revealed that 60 percent of rape victims in the Democratic Republic of Congo were gang raped by armed men and more than half of assaults took place in the family home at night, often in the presence of the victim's husband and children. The majority of rapists were either soldiers or militiamen. The report also shows a seventeenfold increase in rapes carried out by civilians between 2004 and 2008. While 56 percent of assaults were carried out in the home, 16 percent took place in fields and 15 percent in the forest. The report also describes the stigma of rape for the women within their own families. Only 1 percent of women went to the hospital with their husbands. Very few women came for treatment in time to prevent HIV infection. Women are often abandoned by their husbands

---

[22]"Rape: It's a War Crime," *Los Angeles Times,* August 13, 2009, http://articles.latimes.com/2009 /aug/13/opinion/ed-rape13.

[23]Ibid.

due to the stigma caused by sexual assault. Although countries and worldwide organizations have increasingly identified rape as a war crime, the gravity of the problem continues to be minimized with few rapes being prosecuted.[24]

Research supports the need for defining global violence against women and girls in language that echoes other genocides: gendercide. How else can we identify the massive problem of violence inflected on a large population of persons because of their gender alone? Misogyny rooted in historical, cultural and religious belief systems continues to fuel crimes and practices that target women and girls.

A 2005 World Health Organization study reported that nearly one-third of Ethiopian women had been physically forced by a partner to have sex against her will within twelve months of the study.[25] "Honor killings" take the lives of thousands of young women every year, mainly in North Africa, Western Asia and parts of South Asia. The Human Rights Commission of Pakistan reported that 2002 saw a 25 percent increase in "honor killings" of women, with 461 women murdered by family members in 2002 in two provinces (Sindh and Punjab) alone. A study conducted by UNICEF/UNAIDS in 2007 in eastern and southern Africa reported that 17 to 22 percent of girls aged fifteen to nineteen are HIV positive, compared to 3 to 7 percent of boys of similar age. This pattern, seen in many other regions of the world, is evidence that girls are being infected with HIV by a much older group of men. In some communities it is believed that sexual intercourse with a virgin will cure the disease. In Zimbabwe, domestic violence accounts for more than 60 percent of murder cases, and a survey completed in Santiago, Chile, indicates that 80 percent of women have suffered physical, emotional or sexual abuse by a male partner or relative. In South Africa, one in four men has admitted to raping a woman, often as a teenager as

---

[24]"Congo-Kinshasa: New Report Shows Shocking Pattern of Rape in Eastern Congo," Oxfam International press release, April 15, 2010, oxfam.org/en/pressroom/pressrelease/2010-04-15/new-report -shows-shocking-pattern-rape-eastern-congo.

[25]World Health Organization, *Multi-Country Study on Women's Health and Domestic Violence Against Women* (Geneva: WHO, 2005).

a "male rite of passage." Each year sixty million girls are sexually assaulted on their way to school.[26]

The numbers are so overwhelming that Amnesty International depicts a scenario that reduces the global population to a village of one thousand people. In this world village of ours, 500 are women. It should be 510, but 10 were never born because of gender-selective abortions or they died in infancy because of neglect. Of the 500 women, 167 will be beaten or in some other way experience violence in their lifetime and 100 of the women will be victims of rape or attempted rape. This image of our "world village" helps us to grasp the sheer numbers of women and girls affected by violence. However, the numbers do not do justice to the stories of each woman and child sold into slavery or early marriage, held down for an FGM ceremony, raped by an invading soldier, beaten by a husband, burned alive for rejecting an older stranger as her husband or forced to work long hours in a factory for meager pay. Equally heinous are the untold stories of young girls and teens sent to other countries with the hope of becoming employed and helping their families out of dire poverty. They are naive, hopeful and innocent. They soon learn upon arriving at their destinations that they are expected to work as escorts, dancers and prostitutes with little or no pay. Their hope for a future is dimmed and then extinguished.

A triple threat: poverty, violence and disease. There is no causal relationship between violence against women and girls and poverty. However, there is no doubt that poverty is a crushing problem in regions of the world where women are oppressed, denied access to education, and unable to make economic choices for themselves and their children. Women bear the main responsibility for meeting the basic needs of their families in most parts of the world. Yet, they are often denied access to the resources necessary to provide for the basic health care, nutrition and education of their children. The majority of the

---

[26]Gro Harlem Brundtland, "Defeating Discrimination: How to End Violence Against Women," Elders blog, March 8, 2013, http://theelders.org/article/defeating-discrimination-how-end-violence-against-women.

world's poor are women. Two-thirds of the world's illiterate population
are female. There are millions of children not in school, and the majority are girls. Food prices also severely impact women. A significant
percentage of women barely eat once a day and share what they have
with their children. These women suffer the effects of malnutrition,
making it extremely difficult for them to care for their own children
and themselves.[27]

Nicholas Kristof and Sheryl WuDunn describe poverty-fighting
strategies for poor women that have been very effective in raising the
living standards of the poor in Africa and China.[28] There has been a
great migration of rural Chinese women to work in urban factories.
Kristof and WuDunn point out that 80 percent of the assembly-line jobs
in the coastal area of China and 70 percent of similar jobs throughout
the manufacturing belt are held by women. This dramatic geographic
and social change has resulted in increased interest in the education of
girls, allowing women to earn and save money for themselves and their
families, and raising the gross national product and savings rate.[29] While
these job opportunities contribute positively to the status of women in
China, inequalities remain between women and men. Factory jobs are
low paying and the hours are long. During a trip to China and a visit to
one factory that produced fine, colorful embroidery, I was told that all
the workers were women. There were rows of tables with stools with
one small light overhanging each station. Each employee worked eight
to ten hours daily, but I wondered at the physical impact such conditions have on women's hands, eyes and backs.

Supervisors in factory stores are men, and the women on the floor
have no power to negotiate with their customers. They defer to their
male supervisors for negotiating prices with the customers. Women
workers are found not only in factories but also in the large Western-

---

[27]See The Hunger Project, "Know Your World: Facts About Hunger and Poverty," www.thp.org/learn
_more/issues/know_your_world_facts_about_hunger_and_poverty.

[28]Nicholas D. Kristof and Sheryl WuDunn, *Half the Sky: Turning Oppression into Opportunity for Women
Worldwide* (New York: Knopf, 2009), p. xix.

[29]Ibid.

style hotels that now populate Chinese cities. They work as hostesses, maids, desk clerks and waitresses. Employment opportunities and education have lifted many women and girls out of poverty in China. Nevertheless, there still remain economic inequalities and a lack of social freedom for most women and girls. The relationship between poverty and oppression persists. There is hope that as women take their place in the marketplace they will continue to put pressure on the government to change its one-child policy and that employers will increasingly give women more opportunities to gain financial security and equality.

Another example of the close interplay between poverty and violence is in the trafficking of women and children in the global market. The sex-trafficking trade is fueled by poverty. Young girls are sold by their families so that parents can feed their other children. Poor young women eagerly accept overseas jobs as domestic workers or factory workers and move to a foreign country where they don't know the language—only to discover they are enslaved and expected to work as prostitutes or household servants to pay off their traveling debts. Women deceived into overseas jobs to provide for their own children are not only unable to send money home but are often separated from their children for years. Those that are able to return to their communities are often shunned because they have been raped and sexually assaulted and therefore have "shamed" their families. Poverty and misogyny are the brutal instigators in a cycle that includes exploitation, violence and the fracturing of families.

Disease also inhibits the ability of women to care for themselves and their children. In Africa, AIDS has devastated millions of lives. In many areas of the world HIV/AIDS is rapidly becoming a women's disease. In many of the southern African countries, more than three-quarters of all young people living with HIV are women.[30] Of the 22.5 million people in Africa suffering with AIDS (globally the number is a staggering 33

---

[30]World Health Organization, *UNAIDS Report on the Global AIDS Epidemic 2010* (Geneva: WHO, 2010), p. 10.

million), almost 15 million are women and children.[31] For women in their reproductive years (ages fifteen to forty-four), HIV/AIDS is the leading cause of death and disease worldwide.[32] The lack of health education and ability to protect their bodies has left many women HIV positive. Left without health care women die of AIDS leaving their children orphaned.

Violence against women has a major role in the AIDS epidemic. In South Africa one in four girls will be raped by age sixteen, and a woman born in South Africa "has a greater chance of being raped, than learning how to read."[33] If women are not equipped with health-care information, they have no ability to protect themselves if sexually assaulted. Tragically, there is a widespread myth that sex with a baby or young child will cure a man of HIV or AIDS. Carolyn Dempster reported for the BBC that "Baby Tshepang" was just nine months old when she was brutally raped in a South African town in October of 2001.[34] The practice has become more common. Public justice systems in many countries fail to prosecute perpetrators for violence against women and children. Systemic changes are needed for institutional change.

The relationship and cycle of poverty, violence and disease touches millions of women's lives throughout the world. The significance of this relationship lies not in the analysis as much as in the hopeful response that can result from understanding the interconnectedness of these problems. A united church effort to ease the poverty of women and children in one region of the world can empower them to collectively shun traditional practices that continue to oppress and violate their dignity. For example, microfinance organizations help women in dire poverty set up their own small businesses and thereby provide them an opportunity to give their children an education while raising their own

---

[31]Ibid.

[32]"Statistics: Women and HIV/AIDS," Foundation for AIDS Research, www.amfar.org/About-HIV
-and-AIDS/Facts-and-Stats/Statistics--Women-and-HIV-AIDS/.

[33]Carolyn Dempster, "Rape—Silent War on SA Women," *BBC News*, April 9, 2002, http://news.bbc
.co.uk/2/hi/1909220.stm.

[34]Ibid.

standard of living. Money for food increases their families' chances for nourished and healthy children. Increased education and health lead to self-empowerment and rejection of cultural systems that subjugate females. Mothers begin to envision lives of hope for themselves and their children. These changes impact whole communities. Efforts in Africa and other countries to ensure clean water through the installation of wells and filtration systems offer the possibility of decreased infectious diseases, healthier children, irrigation of farms leading to increased food production, and the hope for women and the larger community to improve their overall living standards.

More possibilities for positive change, and decreased violence in the lives of women and girls, occur when the church intervenes anywhere in the cycle of poverty, violence and disease. Each child or woman deserves to be treated with the dignity that the Creator gives to each human life. The Christian church, no matter the denomination, has as its central confession faith in a God that became incarnate and identifies with the abused and marginalized. This has meaning amidst the reality of suffering and oppression. A perspective of the cross is ultimately a foundation for life, hope and freedom. Christians can imagine and hope for the lifting of the yoke of oppression from the backs of women and children because the burden of evil and sin has already been broken on the back of Jesus. The servant church community is called to be in relationship with the suffering Christ in the world. The church needs to actively work to end the religious, political and cultural supports of this horrific global violence.

3

A Short History

The Social, Religious and Political Roots
of Violence Against Women and Girls

In the United States, prior to the 1970s, researchers and practitioners in the social sciences generally accepted the existing societal beliefs that domestic violence was rare. In the *Journal of Marriage and the Family* there was not a single reference to domestic violence between the years 1939 and 1969.[1] When cases of domestic violence came to the researchers' attention, it was assumed that the victim had masochistic tendencies, and consequently the treatment focused on the woman. The victim was perceived to contribute to her own abuse. Descriptions of the victims in the literature include such terms as aggressive, masculine, sexually frigid, hostile and manipulative. Early research in the field reflected the reality of a deeply rooted patriarchal belief system. Cultural and social mores also helped to shape misguided therapeutic interventions and punitive law enforcement response.

> By never condemning the violence, the authors sanctioned it. The husband's main problem is his weakness, not his assaultiveness. Moreover, the woman not only deserved the violence because of her own aggression and coldness, but also needs and causes it for her psychic well-being. If she only fulfilled her feminine role more adequately and demurely, she would not provoke his rage. One could conclude that if

---

[1] Susan Schechter, *Women and Male Violence: The Visions and Struggles of the Battered Women's Movement* (Boston: South End Press, 1982), pp. 21-22.

women were sexually "giving" when their husbands were drinking, never said a public word about being beaten, and certainly never called the police for protection, all would be fine. The stories of thousands of battered women who did just that and were beaten even more brutally belies these conclusions.[2]

Historically, most societies have tolerated physical abuse of women when it occurs within a family setting. The belief that violence within a home is a private matter has roots in past legal sanctions of male dominance within the family. Husbands and fathers had the right to "chastise" wives and children physically.[3] English common law allowed men to beat their wives with a stick that was no wider then one's thumb—hence the term *rule of thumb*. The phrase *battered woman* was not even a part of our vocabulary until 1974.[4]

The entrenched social belief system that entitled men to dominate their partners was not only rooted in the legal system but also in religious belief systems. Volumes have been written on the history of women in the church, and it is not my intention to offer any extensive study on the church's treatment of women. However, it is important to consider the underlying historical attitudes and belief systems that have supported the Christian tradition and teachings regarding women and their influence on the development of law, societal norms and ethics. Negative attitudes toward women have roots in early Christian teachings. Throughout church history there is evidence to support the widespread belief system that provided for the denigration of women. Women were blamed for the fall, believed to be easily deceived by the devil and considered morally, religiously and mortally dangerous to the man who is striving for sexual purity.

RELIGIOUS ROOTS

In examining ancient Christian teaching and statements concerning gender roles, there is the danger of drawing negative anachronistic con-

---

[2]Ibid., p. 22.
[3]Susan Moller Okin, *Justice, Gender, and the Family* (New York: Basic Books, 1989), p. 129.
[4]Schechter, *Women and Male Violence*, p. 16.

clusions that only partially describe the perspective of the architects of Western Christian thought and theology. For example, Augustine's anthropology and profound description of sin and grace and the creative power of God's love are foundational for Luther's understanding of the meaning of a theology of the cross. Nevertheless, it is also important not to ignore the impact of the misogyny that characterized many of these early theologians. The consequences of misogyny shaped an institutional response to women and their role in the church that still lingers in the church today. For example, Augustine believed sex to be inherently evil. Although Augustine acknowledged the necessity of sex for procreation, history scholar Mary Malone argues that Augustine was never able to divorce "intercourse from the realm of sin." Malone maintains that Augustine "struggled with that 'inner corrosion' that was the result of the fall. This was one of the primary sources for his doctrine of original sin and its handing on from generation to generation in the 'hot little act' of intercourse."[5]

The identification of women with sexuality due to their "tempting, seductive nature" became a powerful influence on men's views toward women and on developing church teaching.[6] The fear of women as temptresses, coupled with medieval theology increasingly emphasizing the necessity of works (celibacy was one way to achieve and maintain holiness) for salvation, increasingly silenced women and removed them from public leadership in the church. The proliferation of convents in the medieval era is testament to a theological shift away from a biblically based theology of the cross. However, convent life

---

[5]Mary T. Malone, *Women & Christianity* (Maryknoll, NY: Orbis Books, 2001), 1:154-55. According to Augustine, woman is subject only to God in respect to her intelligence. However, because of her gender and bodily difference from man, she is not complete and therefore is subject to man. See Genevieve Lloyd, "Augustine and Aquinas," in *Feminist Theology: A Reader,* ed. Ann Loades and Karen Armstrong (Louisville: Westminster Press, 1990), pp. 91-92. See also Mary T. Malone's discussion of Augustine, Ambrose and Jerome with regard to the influence of their thought on sexuality in Western Christianity in "The Life of Virginity," in *Women & Christianity,* 1:144-71. However, Augustine recognized the spiritual equality of woman and man. See Augustine, *The City of God,* trans. Marcus Dods (New York: Modern Library, 1993), p. 804.

[6]See Malone, *Women & Christianity,* for a complete and well-documented history of women in the church.

also provided an avenue for women to have some freedom apart from marriage. Unfortunately, marriage was not an attractive option for many women. Women were not allowed to read or write since these skills were not useful for domestic duties. The few exceptions were members of the aristocracy.[7]

> Literacy is one thing; preparation to teach and write theology, philosophy, or literature is something else again. Before the Renaissance there is almost a complete lack of what might be called systematic writing by women. . . . Women had no opportunity to enter the arena of discourse except through the oblique route of relating special revelations from God. It is certainly true that women were not allow to preach or speak publicly outside their convents, unless they were people of truly outstanding audacity and courage.[8]

The Reformation period offered new opportunities for women as a theology based on justification by faith alone began to influence teachings on vocation. Martin Luther's emphasis on the freedom of Christians to live lives in response to the promise of justification undercut any vocational hierarchies based on works. All work was sacred, even the diapering of babies! This theology offered hope to women who poured out of nunneries no longer believing that celibacy was a necessary step toward holiness. This theology had practical ramifications for Luther's own life. He married a former nun, Katherine von Bora, and often deferred to her for translation and the oversight of family finances. He playfully called her "Herr Doktor" in his letters when she was tending some of her own land away from the home. His respect for her as a person in her own right was reflected in his last will, in which he ordered that his property be left under her control. This was indeed a radical move! Women did not own or inherit property at that time, and it was not until the period of late modernity that this was made possible.

Unfortunately, the hope of equality and social and religious freedom

---

[7]Andrew Kadel, *Matrology: A Bibliography of Writings by Christian Women from the First to the Fifteenth Centuries* (New York: Continuum, 1995), p. 20.
[8]Ibid., pp. 21-22.

was not to last. The Reformation and Confessional eras ultimately defined the family in patriarchal terms. The accompanying stipulation that wives submit to husbands continued the tolerance for oppression and even violence without retribution and punishment for most offenders. Challenges to misogynist theology and practice came from both within and outside the church throughout its history. Nevertheless, religious and cultural norms that sanctioned violence against women have strongly influenced law and societal attitudes up to the present.

The Christian history of women is complex. In some places and periods in history women were able to live out their vocations and lives in relative social freedom and had protection from violence. For example, women of the first generation of Christianity were able to demonstrate leadership in the newly formed churches. They were able to accept roles as apostles, deacons, elders and house leaders, and there is evidence that a few were ordained bishops! This posed a radical departure from societal norms. Many of the great medieval women mystics also found avenues to voice their theology and were influential in church and state politics. The nineteenth-century revival and abolitionist movements birthed the first women's movement, with its demands for the vote and individual rights, in the United States. Women evangelists and preachers were given freedom to exercise authority in some churches and in the mission field. Violence against women in the home was a cause taken up by the Women's Temperance Societies as they worked to end what they thought was one cause of wife battering, alcohol abuse. However, although women eventually won the vote and were given greater roles of leadership in the church, and though new developments in biblical hermeneutics revealed new understandings of biblical equality, the stubborn problem of violence against women has remained entrenched in societies and the church.

RECENT DEVELOPMENTS

Oppression and violence against women and girls can be identified in many different historical contexts. The atrocities experienced by women and girls today echo past violent crimes that targeted the vulnerable. Beverly Mitchell, in her book *Plantations and Death Camps,* writes movingly of the particularity of women's suffering during the period of American slavery and the Holocaust. The vulnerability of black slave women ensured that they were "at the whim and debased desires" of white male slave owners. Jewish women also experienced the humiliation of sexual advances, strip searches and assaults from camp guards.[9] The atrocities committed against Jewish and African American women and girls during slavery and the Holocaust resulted in untold numbers maimed, tortured and dead. Systematic violence against women and girls remains a "holocaust" in many areas of the world, and rape as a tool of war is a perennial problem and outrage.

During the 1970s in the United States, the second feminist movement created a grassroots group of women who gathered together over the concerns that abused women in local communities were not being offered safe shelter, legal resources and protection.[10] During this period there began a paradigm shift from viewing violence against women as a family issue, and therefore private, to viewing it as a criminal and public concern. In the legal realm, domestic violence began to be viewed as a political construct and social problem. Through the pioneering work of battered women's shelters and batterer intervention programs, enormous educational efforts were made in the courts and communities to hold perpetrators accountable for their actions. Guidelines for courts and batterer intervention programs were adopted by many states. These guidelines are based on the understanding of gender violence as a behavioral issue that needs to be addressed not only by the perpetrator but by the whole community. The language of intervention, versus counseling, is often used to emphasize the need for a societal response rather than an individualistic, psychological one. In many parts of the country the courts, rather than the family counselor

---

[9]Beverly Eileen Mitchell, *Plantations and Death Camps: Religion, Ideology, and Human Dignity* (Minneapolis: Fortress, 2009), pp. 16-17.

[10]See Schechter, *Women and Male Violence.* This text offers a concise history and analysis of the early stages of the battered women's movement.

or pastor, are first to intervene in domestic violence situations.[11]

The belief system that was centered on blaming the victim began to change slowly as grassroots women's groups across the United States and worldwide called for the sheltering and support of battered women. Women began to find safe shelter in their local communities; advocates also began to demand that the perpetrators of violence be held accountable in the courts. The criminalization of domestic violence spawned new intervention programs targeting abusers and mandatory training of police, victim advocates, prosecutors and judges.

Crisis hotlines, legal aid services, counseling and victim advocacy were provided in communities and increasingly became financially supported by the government. The original Violence Against Women Act (VAWA), enacted in 1994 as Title IV of the Violent Crime Control and Law Enforcement Act (Pub. L. No. 103-322), established within the Department of Justice and Health and Human Services discretionary grant programs for state, local and Indian tribal governments. These funds were significant in both providing federal funding for shelter services and identifying violence against women as a serious health and societal problem. Psychological language used to blame victims was now being replaced by legal language used to hold perpetrators accountable. VAWA was reauthorized by Congress in 2000 and expanded to include funding for combating sexual assault, stalking and dating violence.

Christian churches in the United States were marginally represented in these late-twentieth-century efforts to end violence against women. Some offered referrals and support to women victims while others continued to blame women for the abuse they experienced. My first encounter with this tension between battered women advocates and Christian churches came soon after I was hired as a battered women's program director in a small northeastern city. Our program offered abused women and their children services that included shelter, legal advocacy services, counseling and support. Soon after becoming director I received a call from a local pastor regarding a woman who attended his

---

[11]Ibid.

church. His first words to me were, "You are obviously not a Christian or you would not be breaking up families in this community!" Sadly, I was not surprised by this declaration. I had already encountered suspicion from other Christian leaders regarding my work on behalf of abused women, and had even been accused by pastors of being "anti-male." I soon realized through my engagement with Christian churches that the very work of helping to empower and educate women with regard to their inherent dignity and right to life and safety was a threat to those that believed in a patriarchal system as a means to hold onto power.

In the early 1990s I faced opposition within my own church when I proposed that we offer a support group for abused women within the church community. My pastor, although sympathetic to battered women "outside the church," stated that there was no need for such a group within the church because there were no abused women within his congregation! I later began a church group on "relationship issues." Seated around the table were battered women and victims of child molestation. These Christian women were grateful to be able finally to tell their stories, which they had kept hidden for so many years. Recently, a student reported that the pastor of a church in which he was interning counseled a physically abused wife in the congregation to "cooperate in the bedroom" as one way to end the abuse in the marriage. Christian pastors may be reluctant to refer to "secular" women shelters and counseling centers. Consequently, they attempt to counsel, with little or no training, families impacted by violence.

The same distrust existed for battered women advocates, who thought that Christian leaders undermined their work. I experienced their fear as a reality throughout my fifteen years of working within programs that were trying to help abused women. One executive director took me out to lunch to discuss the fact that I was a Christian. She wanted to know how I could possibly do this advocacy work and be a Christian at the same time! She had never witnessed any church support in the community for the work of helping battered women. This lack of understanding and relationship between many churches and battered women advocates in the 1980s through the 1990s was slow to change but has gained positive movement during the past decade. More and more shelter programs are realizing the importance of partnering with churches to improve the lives of women, and, increasingly, churches understand the value of the services offered by battered women advocates. Recently I was invited to be on a panel consisting of local religious leaders to address the staff of a local battered women's shelter on issues of faith and violence against women. The vice executive director of the agency commented to me that this was the first training of staff on this topic. The dialogue was helpful to both the religious trainers and the agency staff. This exchange was a positive change and revealed progress in the relationship between local churches and women's programs. Nevertheless, there is much work to be done in increasing communication and in the sharing of resources between churches and community organizations.

Feminist theologians and advocates were the first to identify violence against women as a legal and health issue. Many church leaders are not only acknowledging this as a critical issue to be addressed but are also working with advocates to educate their local communities. However, owing to the church's history and, paradoxically, the loss of the centrality of a theology of the cross, limited definitions of violence against women and girls and inadequate responses remain problematic in the Christian churches.

VIOLENCE AGAINST WOMEN AND GIRLS AS AN INTERNATIONAL HUMAN RIGHTS PROBLEM

Violence against women and girls in the United States occurs predominantly within the family constellation. Approximately 1.3 million women have been abused during the past year, and the health-care costs continue to rise.[12] Violence against females, both within and outside of

---

[12]Michele Bograd, "Feminist Perspectives on Wife Abuse: An Introduction," in *Feminist Perspectives on Wife Abuse,* ed. Kersti Yllö and Michele Bograd (Newbury Park, CA: Sage, 1988), pp. 11-26. In 1975, the National Organization for Women formed a task force on battered women. In 1978, the National Coalition Against Domestic Violence (NCADV) was formed in Washington, DC. The first national

the United States, is a significant and complex global human rights problem that exacerbates the problems of poverty and communicable diseases such as AIDS. Violence against women and girls has not been a focus of concern for the international community until very recently. The widespread acceptance of patriarchal systems and other systemic causes of institutionalized violence against women and girls has led to a lack of action and change within many countries. International organizations that were concerned about human rights did not concentrate their efforts in this area until the 1990s.

The argument for reframing the problem of domestic violence as a human rights issue centers primarily on the attempt to heighten the gravity of the problem. Viewing this type of violence as a human rights issue presents a more *holistic* perspective, taking into account a wide range of related issues. In the United States, where issues are often compartmentalized and isolated from one another, a holistic perspective is particularly important.[13] The Universal Declaration of Human Rights adopted by the United Nations General Assembly in 1948 asserts that every human being has the right to life, liberty, and security of the person, equal pay for equal work, a standard of living adequate for health and well-being, education, freedom from slavery, and equal protection of the law.[14] The violation of women's dignity and personal safety relates to each

---

membership conference was held in 1980. Emerging state coalitions developed the shelter movement, which created safe homes for battered women and their children. Literature from the movement after 1975 reflects the growing trend shifting from the medical model to the current sociopolitical view of male hierarchical domination as the cause of violence against women. See also Ginny NiCarthy, Karen Merriam and Sandra Coffman, *Talking It Out: A Guide to Groups for Abused Women* (Seattle: Seal Press, 1984); Schechter, *Women and Male Violence*; Del Martin, *Battered Wives* (San Francisco: Glide, 1976); Lenore E. Walker, *The Battered Woman* (New York: Harper & Row, 1979). Statistics have been compiled by the National Coalition Against Domestic Violence, www.ncadv.org/files/DomesticViolenceFactSheet(National).

[13]Carrie Cuthbert, Mala Rafik and Kim Slote (staff of the Women's Rights Network) in a letter to Sara K. Gould, Vice President for Program, Ms. Foundation for Women, New York, NY, January 30, 1998.

[14]Text from the Universal Declaration of Human Rights, summarized in Julie Mertus, "Our Human Rights: A Manual for Women's Human Rights," unpublished article distributed for comments in the Fourth UN World Conference for Women, Beijing, China, August 1995. According to Bonnie Campbell, United States Department of Justice, in a speech given October 1996 at the University of Massachusetts at Dartmouth, the Universal Declaration of Human Rights is an important tool that is recognized internationally in the effort to end domestic violence. It has only recently been adopted as a tool and strategy for this effort in the United States.

area on the United Nations list. Familial violence is but one type of a wide range of gender-based crimes against women, crimes that include torture, confinement either physically or psychologically through terror and threats, involuntary prostitution, and pornography.

Defining violence against women and girls that occurs in the home as a human rights issue ensures its high visibility. Historically, domestic violence has been seen as a private issue; therefore, changes in laws and enforcement of existing laws prohibiting abuse against women have been slow and difficult. Defining domestic violence as a human rights issue exposes "private" violence as a legitimate public crime and a community problem. It highlights the causal relationship between domestic violence and the denial of women's human rights.

When women are denied human rights in private, their human rights in the public sphere also suffer since what occurs in private shapes their ability to participate fully in the public arena. For example, in some countries state policies deny women the right to travel or leave the country without approval from their fathers, their husbands, their brothers or even their sons. Few of those who have protested their governments' refusal to allow people to leave their countries have recognized this as a form of violence. Other women cannot exercise their right to freedom of assembly by attending political meetings or participating in development projects without fear of being beaten or locked up by their partners. Such violations are reported regularly, yet there is not an outcry in the name of human rights about the denial of these women's right to political participation, to assembly, to free speech and to citizenship.[15] In many parts of the world women and girls who are sexually assaulted and raped are rejected by their families and communities. They are blamed for their own victimization. They are assaulted and then shamed. The violence perpetrated in private reduces their power in the public realm.

The reframing of domestic violence as a human rights issue is a recent

---

[15]Charlotte Bunch, "Transforming Human Rights from a Feminist Perspective," in *Women's Rights: Human Rights,* ed. Julie Peters and Andrea Wolper (New York: Routledge, 1995), p. 14.

development in the United States, but it is not a new concept in many parts of the world. Friedman describes the emergence of human rights activities in Latin America during its many dictatorships as involving masses of women. The Madres de la Plaza de Mayo demanded the return of their children who had disappeared in Argentina during the Dirty War under the military dictatorship in power from 1976 to 1983. The mothers' visible opposition made the issue public and political. These mothers worked not only for the return of their children but for a change in their social and political status. Although the political climate shifted, the lasting changes that were hoped for were not fulfilled. Women's issues remained marginalized.[16] Nevertheless, the cries of the Madres impressed upon the international community the need for greater visibility of women's needs and the lack of protection of their rights as human beings and citizens. Women in India, Africa, Pakistan, Ghana and Sudan organized and made public other gender-based crimes while demanding full human rights. Reports from a wide range of women's groups indicate an increased level of grassroots activities by women working to end atrocities.

Women have worked within their own political contexts during international conferences sponsored by the United Nations. The United Nations designated 1975 to 1985 the Decade for Women as a way to focus on issues particular to women globally. Within this time period women's issues were placed on international intergovernmental agendas. Women participated in official delegations of the General Assembly in three meetings during the decade (Mexico City in 1975, Copenhagen in 1980 and Nairobi in 1985). Their participation in the Non-Governmental Forums that accompanied each meeting was crucial. Women were able to develop strategies and plan long-term goals.[17] The documents that emerged throughout this time period and that are most relevant to the issue of domestic violence include the Convention on the Elimination

---

[16]Elisabeth Friedman, "Women's Human Rights: The Emergence of a Movement," in Peters and Wolper, *Women's Rights: Human Rights*, pp. 21-22.
[17]Ibid., p. 23.

of All Forms of Discrimination Against Women (CEDAW, 1979), the Vienna Declaration and Programme of Action (1993) and the Declaration on the Elimination of Violence Against Women (1993). These statements established gender-based violence as a human rights issue and urged states to eradicate violence against women through enforcement of declared statutes. CEDAW outlined the tasks that states have to undertake to promote women's equality in every area of life.[18] CEDAW was also the first document to acknowledge that discrimination against women exists in many forms:

> The States Parties to the present Convention,
>
> Noting that the Charter of the United Nations reaffirms faith in fundamental human rights, in the dignity and worth of the human persons and in the equal rights of men and women,
>
> Noting that the Universal Declaration of Human Rights affirms the principle of the inadmissibility of discrimination and proclaims that all human beings are born free and equal in dignity and rights and that everyone is entitled to all the rights and freedoms set forth therein, without distinction of any kind, including distinction based on sex,
>
> Noting that States Parties to the International Covenants on Human Rights have the obligation to ensure the equal rights of men and women to enjoy all economic, social, cultural, civil and political rights.[19]

The document also officially recognized the relationship of gender inequality to racism. The eradication of apartheid, all forms of racism and racial discrimination, and colonialism is considered "essential" to the rights of both women and men. What is of particular significance for increasing the legal response to violence against women and girls is contained in article two of the document. Article two condemns all forms of discrimination against women and offers political legal mandates to ensure women's freedom.

---

[18]Women's Rights Network, section 2A.

[19]Excerpt from the preamble to Convention on the Elimination of All Forms of Discrimination Against Women (CEDAW), adopted by the United Nations General Assembly, December 18, 1979, www .un.org/womenwatch/daw/cedaw/text/econvention.htm.

States Parties condemn discrimination against women in all its forms, agree to pursue by all appropriate means and without delay a policy of eliminating discrimination against women and, to this end, undertake:

(a) To embody the principle of the equality of men and women in their national constitutions or other appropriate legislation if not yet incorporated therein and to ensure, through law and other appropriate means, the practical realization of this principle;

(b) To adopt appropriate legislative and other measures, including sanctions where appropriate, prohibiting all discrimination against women;

(c) To establish legal protection of the rights of women on an equal basis with men and to ensure through competent national tribunals and other public institutions the effective protection of women against any act of discrimination;

(d) To refrain from engaging in any act or practice of discrimination against women and to ensure that public authorities and institutions shall act in conformity with this obligation;

(e) To take all appropriate measures to eliminate discrimination against women by any person, organization or enterprise;

(f) To take all appropriate measures, including legislation, to modify or abolish existing laws, regulations, customs and practices which constitute discrimination against women;

(g) To repeal all national penal provisions which constitute discrimination against women.[20]

In addition "States Parties" are mandated to implement legislation "for the purpose of guaranteeing them the exercise and enjoyment of human rights and fundamental freedoms on a basis of equality with men."[21]

In 1992, the United Nations Committee on the Elimination of Discrimination Against Women prepared general comments and recommendations on the CEDAW document from 1979. It is interesting to note that the committee clarified the role of "private" violence in the previous document. First, their comments clearly outlined the relationship of vio-

---

[20]CEDAW, article 2. Article 2 of CEDAW addresses the need for legal and political penalties for violations of women's human rights.
[21]CEDAW, article 3.

lence committed by persons known to the victim to violence perpetrated by the state or objective persons. Second, they condemned gender-based violence in all its various forms whether committed by family members or by persons unknown to the victim. The CEDAW document applies to violence perpetrated by public authorities. Such acts of violence may breach that state's obligation under general international human rights law and under other conventions, in additional to breaching this convention. The 1992 committee emphasized, however, that discrimination under the convention is not restricted to action by or on behalf of governments. For example, under article 2(e), the CEDAW called on state parties to take all appropriate measures to eliminate discrimination against women by any person, organization or enterprise. Under general international law and specific human rights conventions, states may also be responsible for private acts if they fail to act with due diligence to prevent violations of rights or to investigate and punish acts of violence, and to provide compensation to victims.

Third, the committee made specific recommendations for addressing violence against women, including family violence:

(r) Measures that are necessary to overcome family violence should include:

(i) Criminal penalties where necessary and civil remedies in case of domestic violence;

(ii) Legislation to remove the defence of honour in regard to the assault or murder of a female family member;

(iii) Services to ensure the safety and security of victims of family violence, including refugees, counselling and rehabilitation programmes;

(iv) Rehabilitation programmes for perpetrators of domestic violence;

(v) Support services for families where incest or sexual abuse has occurred; . . .

(u) States parties should report on all forms of gender-based violence, and such reports should include all available data on the incidence of each form of violence and on the effects of such violence on the women who are victims;

(v) The reports of States parties should include information on the legal, preventive and protective measures that have been taken to overcome violence against women, and on the effectiveness of such measures.[22]

One hundred fifty nations have ratified CEDAW. President Carter signed CEDAW on behalf of the United States in 1979, but the US is the only major industrialized nation that has not ratified this United Nations document.

The Vienna Declaration (1993) that was issued from the UN World Conference on Human Rights most explicitly recognizes violence against women in both the private and public arena as a human rights issue.

18. The human rights of women and of the girl-child are an inalienable, integral and indivisible part of universal human rights. The full and equal participation of women in political, civil, economic, social and cultural life, at the national, regional and international levels, and the eradication of all forms of discrimination on grounds of sex are priority objectives of the international community. . . .

The human rights of women should form an integral part of the United Nations human rights activities, including the promotion of all human rights instruments relating to women.

The World Conference on Human Rights urges Governments, institutions, intergovernmental and non-governmental organizations to intensify their efforts for the protection and promotion of all human rights of women and the girl-child.[23]

As a result of the Vienna conference, a special rapporteur on violence against women was named in order to integrate women's concerns into every area of the United Nations' theater of operations. It is historically significant that the Vienna conference explicitly defined domestic violence and all other forms of violence against women and girls as human rights issues.

---

[22]UN Division for the Advancement of Women: Department of Economic and Social Affairs, General Comments and Recommendations of the UN Treaty Bodies, Committee on the Elimination of Discrimination Against Women, General Recommendation No. 19 (Eleventh Session, 1992), Special Recommendation 24.r, u and v, www.un.org/womenwatch/daw/cedaw/recommendations/recomm .htm. See also Women's Human Rights, section 3A for commentary on recommendations.

[23]Vienna Declaration and Programme of Action, adopted at the World Conference on Human Rights, June 25, 1993, www.ohchr.org/EN/ProfessionalInterest/Pages/Vienna.aspx.

Because the Vienna Declaration was accepted by the Human Rights Conference, all members of the United Nations were required to accept the statement. Nevertheless, legal protection for women and girls was a strong recommendation, not a mandate. The conference body also refused to summon an investigation, called for by the Women's Caucus, into the socioeconomic causes of gender-based violence. The members also rejected a proposal to add gender discrimination wherever racism was mentioned in the declaration. Violence against women was still not perceived to be a problem of gender discrimination worthy of being addressed with the same degree of gravity as racism.

In December 1993, the United Nations adopted the Declaration on the Elimination of Violence Against Women. This was a direct result of the global work of women and human rights advocates as evidenced by the presentation and adoption of the Vienna Declaration in June of that same year. "This Declaration defines for the first time what constitutes an act of violence against women and calls on governments and the international community to take specific measures to prevent such acts."[24]

THE CHURCH AND HUMAN RIGHTS

Many Christian churches continue to address many social issues in theological and legal terms, and they have more recently used the language of human rights to describe many global social problems. Nevertheless, there have been little reflection and work within the Christian community toward regarding violence against women and girls as a human rights issue. Therefore, it is important to examine, at least in a summary manner, the relationship of human rights language and concepts and theology. Early work done by other religious bodies, including the World Council of Churches (WCC), provided a foundation for later work by church bodies. For example, a Lutheran conference sponsored by the Department of Studies of the Lutheran World Federation that

---

[24]Gayle Kirshenbaum, "After Victory, Women's Human Rights Movement Takes Stock," *Ms. Magazine*, 4.2 (September/October 1993): 20.

met June 29 through July 3, 1976, examined the results of the 1974 Consultation on Human Rights of the World Council of Churches and the study "Theological Bases of Human Rights" written by the World Alliance of Reformed Churches (WARC). Participants of this conference focused on the theological implication of human rights from the Lutheran perspective.

A paper presented at the conference by Heinz-Eduard Tödt is particularly relevant because it summarizes well various theological positions on the issue of human rights. Tödt also refers to the relationship between the codified legal human rights that had been ratified by members of the United Nations and human rights promoted and formulated in discussion in the churches and among theologians. He concludes that there is no real difference between universal postulates on human rights capable of being formulated in the discussion in the churches and among theologians and the codified human rights agreements of the United Nations.[25] The latter holds legal significance that can serve as a tool for the church. One dominant theological view of human rights that Tödt describes is best represented by that of Jürgen Moltmann. Tödt describes Moltmann's commentary on the WARC document as starting with the "basic salvation history affirmations about God's covenant with his people, his liberating deeds, and the place of law in this history."[26] A person's rights and freedom are made possible by God's covenant with his people.

From the perspective of a theology of the cross, it is the doctrine of justification that provides the lens for viewing human rights. The righteousness received by grace through faith reaffirms human dignity because of the new relationship to God through Christ. It is on the foundation of creation that this dignity extends to all humankind. Through

---

[25]Heinz-Eduard Tödt, "Theological Reflections on the Foundations of Human Rights," *Lutheran World* 24, no. 1 (1977): 46. Tödt also notes that human rights consist of three essential elements: freedom, equality and participation (p. 48). This is particularly relevant for defining domestic violence as a human rights issue in the legal realm. Violence against women interferes with all three rights, but especially the right to equality.

[26]Ibid., p. 52.

the intimacy of being created *imago dei,* the gifts of life and dignity are bestowed on each person. The incarnation is also evidence of this deep personal intimacy. God chose to be born into the ordinariness of the life of humankind. God's revelation through creation, the incarnation and the cross provides the underlying foundation for a theological view of human rights. The hidden revelation of Christ made evident through the incarnation and cross is reflective of the nature of a God who is concerned with the inherent condition of humanity. The suffering, the poor, the oppressed—all have dignity because God has created and identified with those who have no dignity before evil and corruption. The gospel is the foundation for human rights.[27] The basic precept of the golden rule has within it the core foundation for equality of persons and the right of human dignity. Therefore, there is no need to provide a further theological basis for human rights. The language of human rights and their already established status are secular tools useful for justice work. These laws are viable instruments to be used by Christians. God's acceptance of humanity through Christ allows God to be God and the person to live out humanity in fullness. The task at hand then is not to create a Christian image of human beings but to "engage in the concrete struggle for more humanity."[28]

Nevertheless, an argument can be made for biblical support in the use of the language of human rights. The phrase *human rights* has its modern roots in the Enlightenment, *les droits des l'homme,* and is not a biblical term. Biblical themes support the Christian concern of human rights and the dignity of all persons.[29] The defense of the weak against

---

[27]Gunter Krüsche, "Human Rights in a Theological Perspective: A Contribution from the GDR," *Lutheran World* 24, no. 1 (1977): 60. Krüsche notes that even in the field of Catholic theology, where there are the usual natural law arguments for ethical norms, the gospel is the basis for promoting action in the area of human rights. He quotes, "We Christians also find in the gospel the deepest motive for our involvement in the defense and promotion of human rights—the gospel constrains us to do so" (Episcopal Synod, Rome, October 23, 1974).

[28]Foster R. McCurley and John H. Reumann, "Human Rights in the Law and Romans (Series A)," in *Human Rights: Rhetoric or Reality,* ed. George W. Forell and William H. Lazareth (Philadelphia: Fortress, 1978), p. 17.

[29]Ibid., p. 22. See pp. 18-22 for a thorough discussion of the eight biblical themes that support the use of human rights language.

the strong is a Christian mandate. Although the language of "human rights" is not used frequently, it is present. Isaiah exclaims:

> Ah, you who make iniquitous decrees,
>   who write oppressive statues,
> to turn aside the needy from justice
>   and to rob the poor of my people of their right [*mishpat*],
> that widows may be your spoil,
>   and that you may make the orphans your prey! (Is 10:1-2)

The Lord does not approve when "a person's right" is rejected (see Lam 3:34-36). The connection of human rights to biblical justice needs to be more explicit within the churches in order to help Christians understand the relationship between global problems that violate persons' rights to equality and life and to provide tools to help the churches engage in the struggle to uphold the dignity of all peoples.

The use of human rights language is helpful for churches because it describes the intersection between different social issues that are often compartmentalized into separate political issues. Basic rights to shelter, food and health care, for example, are often viewed from differing political positions rather than seen as components of the same basic right to life. Rights language is also useful because it is the universal global language understood by most people of differing religious, social and racial backgrounds. For example, domestic violence in the United States can be connected more easily to other forms of violence against women because it is rooted in the same sins of misogyny and legal human rights violations such as the right to life and equality. Christians understand these rights as integral to the gifts of life and human dignity given by God the Creator. Nevertheless, the reality of injustice calls for a common language of understanding that defines these sins that violate the dignity of humanity in order to tie together social issues and have a consistent vision of justice.

Examples of the theological use of human rights language are the teaching of Pope John XXIII and Vatican II, Pope Paul VI, and the theological development of human rights by Pope John Paul II. These three men argued that human rights language be used as a tool to describe the relationship of biblical justice and God's mission. Pope John Paul II, in commenting on the horror of the Holocaust, stated that "the only way to avoid another disaster like Nazi Germany was to teach 'a new spirit, the spirit of the rights of the human person, the rights of nations, of international justice and solidarity.'"[30] A comprehensive "charter of rights" was first expressed in Pope John XXIII's encyclical letter of 1963, *Pacem in Terris*. Here he details the rights of each person that must be honored, including the right to life, the right to bodily integrity, the right to the means necessary for the proper development of life, the right to a just wage and the right to freedom of movement, to name but a few.[31] These rights that Pope John XXIII delineated are based both in God's gift of life and are confirmed by human reason. Rights given are also tied together with the obligations and duties to care for the other. This is very similar in concept to Martin Luther's dialectic of freedom and obligation to others and Dietrich Bonhoeffer's description of costly grace.

The human rights language used to define the many global social problems that all churches must address is a language that is understood universally, connects the relevant social ills together and creates a foundation for a unified church response to violence against women and girls, economic oppression and a host of other social problems. It is important that the church support the work of international organizations that are committed to securing the rights and dignity of women and girls, and of all persons. Theological discrimination from a perspective of a theology of the cross is essential in understanding the relation between the role of the church and human rights. Through theological reflection we can distinguish between the ultimate and

---

[30]Pope John Paul II, quoted by Ted Keating in "Catholic Social Teaching and the Universal Declaration on Human Rights," *Catholic Peace Voice* 23, no. 213 (Spring/Summer 1998), reprinted at www.hrusa .org/advocacy/community-faith/catholic1.shtm.

[31]John XXIII, "*Pacem in Terris*: Encyclical of Pope John XXIII on Establishing Universal Peace in Truth, Justice, Charity, and Liberty," Rome, April 11, 1963, www.vatican.va/holy_father/john_xxiii/encyc licals/documents/hf_j-xxiii_enc_11041963_pacem_en.html.

penultimate, between gospel and law. However, there is always a dialectical tension between the two tasks of the church, *kerygma* and *diakonia*. If this distinction is not maintained, there is a danger that the
church preaches a salvation of "cheap grace," that is, freedom without
service or a gospel of salvation through works. Codified human rights
cannot replace the gospel. Churches that align their theology too
closely with universal rights lose their distinctive Christian identity in
the world. They become another social change agency or humanitarian
relief service. Churches that are concerned only with the ultimate and
fail to promote justice in this world also fail to proclaim the whole of
the gospel. Providing a *theological understanding* of human rights in
order to better utilize established legal codes rather than creating a
theological basis for human rights maintains the dialectical tension
between law and gospel. This view is consistent with Dietrich Bonhoeffer's perennial question, "Who is Christ for us today?" The task of theology is to interpret and proclaim the gospel in today's historical, social
and political context.

The contributions of human rights organizations, documents and
treatises that affirm basic rights to freedom, equality and participation
are important instruments that the church can effectively employ in its
justice work. In the area of violence against women and girls, these instruments provide a definition and framework for viewing the issue in
a large and more global context. They serve to uncover the private violations of women's dignity and reveal violence as a public issue related to
other forms of discrimination against women. The issue of gendercide
becomes more difficult to minimize and marginalize as the focus shifts
from viewing it as a family or private relational violation of rights to
viewing it as an institutional and legal violation of rights.

A human rights approach provides the definition and some excellent
tools for the work establishing full freedom, equality and participation
of women in the human community. However, this approach does not
provide a theological foundation on which the church can then find
direction and meaning for its mission in this area of work. Neither does

a theological base need to be developed in order to support the usefulness of these tools. From the perspective of a theology of the cross, secular methods can be valued as one means of obstructing evil and promoting justice.

Nevertheless, becoming educated in the language and usefulness of human rights and other methodologies is not enough for the church. The work to end gendercide begins with the embracing of the very identity and confession of our faith. The primary task of theology is to proclaim the gospel. Understanding the meaning of this task then shapes the church's *holistic* mission in the world today. The church's mission and ecclesiology are shaped by Christology. It is this centeredness in Christ that is the source and end of all power. The hidden work of Christ at work in the church continues to be alive with hope for the healing and restoration of the oppressed in this world. The mission of the church involves the ethical demand of Christ to identify with and serve the poor. The use of human rights language is a helpful and unifying tool allowing the churches to join with others who are engaged in the work to end the destruction of human lives. However, *diakonia* is always in relation to *kerygma*. Confession of the faith, as Bonhoeffer repeatedly pointed out, must lead to resistance to evil. His cry "church be the church!" was a plea for the *entire* church to embrace its responsibility to *act from* the faith it confessed. It is this crossroads of faith and ethics as a foundation for the work of ending violence against women and girls that is at the heart of a theology of the cross.

- 4 -

The Cross and the Promise

God for Us

If Christ had come with trumpets sounding; if he had a cradle of gold,
His birth would have been a stately thing. But it wouldn't comfort me.
So, He had to lie in a poor girl's lap and be scarcely noticed by
the world. In that lap I can come to see Him; In this way
He now reveals Himself to the distressed.

Yes, He would've had greater fame, if He'd have come in great power,
splendor, wisdom and high class. Yet, He will come some day,
in another way, when He comes to oppose the great nobles.
But now He comes to the poor, who need a Savior.
Then He will come as judge to oppose
those who oppress the poor now.

Martin Luther, 1530

I decided to know nothing among you except
Jesus Christ, and him crucified.

1 Corinthians 2:2

INTRODUCTION

It is important to clearly delineate a theological perspective that is helpful in addressing violence against women and girls before suggesting specific church responses. Carter Lindberg's scholarship in the area of Reformation theology and poor relief is valuable in clarifying the important role that theology holds in shaping an ethical response to contemporary social problems. Lindberg argues that the dialectic of law and gospel cannot be overestimated in determining the relationship of a theology of the cross to the penultimate work of caring for one's neighbor.

> The specifics of Luther's economic and social programs are not directly translatable to the present, but his point of departure— doctrine—is a salutary reminder to contemporary theologians and social advocates in the churches of the indispensable theological foundation for social ethics.[1]

A theology of the cross is rooted in the self-giving act of Jesus on the cross. This theology does not negate the importance of other theologies, particularly liberation theologies, but shifts the center of ethics from human experience to the *theologia crucis*. It does not exclude the sociological concerns of feminist and liberation theologies but rather provides a broader paradigm for addressing those concerns, and includes a response to the oppression of women and girls. Suffering as a result of violence is Christ's suffering. The cross and resurrection of Jesus constitute the central historical event that gives power and meaning to the work of justice building and peacemaking. The cross is the living, breathing proclamation of Christ that demands and shapes the church's ethical response. The way of God, hidden and known only through suffering and the cross, is an invitation to join Christ's mission to heal, to bind up the brokenhearted and to free those who are oppressed.

This perspective maintains that the reality of Christian ethics is

---

[1]Carter Lindberg, *Beyond Charity: Reformation Initiatives for the Poor* (Minneapolis: Augsburg Fortress, 1993), p. 167.

formed by the promise of Christ given to us through the crucified and risen one. Christians, therefore, don't encounter Christ and then go out and serve in order to earn holiness. There is also no need to create a Christian culture. Rather, it is Christ who encounters us through the incarnation, offers the gift of salvation, and ministers through the church and the world to resist evil and promote life and justice. The theological shift from a self-focused superspiritualism to a Christ-centered incarnational theology of the cross is certainly freeing when facing the task of working to end injustice in the world. It is God's ongoing work of creation that we enter into when we enter into relationship with others and work for justice. Care for others includes concern for ending the political, cultural and systemic supports for violence.

This revelation of God *pro nobis* is both the shocking and the reassuring source of all faith, freedom and joy. If by this act salvation is given to those who receive it as the ultimate gift already given, then the language of covenant becomes the language of promise. Because of what Christ has done, *therefore* the believer is set free and all has changed. Salvation is gained not by good works, not by exercising one's giftedness or talents, and not by well-intentioned efforts to make the world better, but rather by this one act already accomplished. As Martin Luther proclaimed incessantly, salvation is freely offered, not achieved by experience, moral duty or reason. The Reformation theme of "justification by faith" is helpful for the church today in offering understanding and depth to the theological and ethical themes of freedom, reconciliation, suffering, relationship of faith and works, and, in general, how a Christian is to live out a life of service to his or her neighbor. At the cross, the church realizes its weakness and dependence on Christ. Here we grasp how God works within the world in unexpected and hidden ways. A theology of the cross and resurrection provides an approach for the church to address social concerns and, particularly, the current global crisis of gendercide.

This confession of the faith is a necessary reminder to a contemporary church that is drawn into the cultural temptation to center itself on its own needs and its giftedness to meet those needs. Christian freedom is misunderstood by the modern interpretation (particularly in American society) of freedom as individual rights and license to do as one pleases. This is in opposition to the freedom centered on the cross. Freedom viewed through the lens of the cross is always in relation to God and the other. It is a freedom to be *for* the other as God has acted *for* us. It is a relational term and a dynamic one. The emphasis on identifying strengths as a step in solving problems is in contrast to the gospel that upended this theology of anthropological positivism and replaced it with a theology of the cross. This gospel describes God's power as being made evident in human weakness. The emphasis on leadership and spirituality in the church today is often a result of the modern propensity toward self-achievement. Self-help books, church growth movements and spiritual-development programs often result from the desire to achieve a closer relationship to God and others through self-focused efforts. These may be well intentioned. Nevertheless, Christ's call to die to the self, pick up the cross and follow is the primary mission required of the church. If Christ is the starting place for the mission of the church, then it is vital to have an ontological perspective for addressing social ethics and the problem of global violence against women and girls. Who Christ is for us *today* shapes the church's agenda in the world. And Christ's agenda requires the attention of the *whole* of the church. This theology of the cross undercuts all self-focused efforts at achievement as surely as Luther's cry of *sola crucis* undercut all medieval theologies of achievement piety.

Therefore, a theology of the cross is not a subject for analysis but rather a perspective, or a path, for believers marked by humility, death to self and devotion to a Savior hidden by suffering. The freedom offered by way of the cross from death and sin is in essence the call to death of self and life in Christ and for others. The command of Jesus to "follow me," spoken to the disciples, led ultimately to the cross of Jesus. It is through the reality of Jesus' death and resurrection that freedom was gained. This freedom, however, was in no way like the freedom of the self, characterized by self-interest. It is a freedom devoted to service for the other. A theology of the cross offers a way out of prideful attempts at self-achievement to complete devotion to the hidden Christ of the poor. The cross's revelation of God's nature is profound for the Christian community. The hidden God of the cross is known through discipleship, that is, a living out of life for the other. Intimacy with this Christ of the cross is the source then for social and political action.

Given the complexity and widespread problem of violence against women and girls, it would seem reasonable for the church to start with an analysis of the problem, to decide on the strategy and resources needed to address this global issue, and then to act toward that end. All those components are needed. In fact, the contributions of feminist theologies in these areas are invaluable. Nevertheless, the starting point for the church should not be with analysis but rather at the foot of the cross. The modern sociological approach has been the predominant one for the church, but it only leads to a partial response centered on a call to become more educated and then to act on this knowledge. Theological reflection on the cross, and the hope and power of the resurrection as foundational, leads to a defining of the problem as a confessional issue that impacts the *whole* of the church and demands a holistic church response. The orientation, analysis, responsibility and response to gendercide shift from a partial response based on experience, knowledge and reason to a holistic response that has to do with the very core identity and mission of the church. Is Paul's declaration that "I decided to know nothing among you except Jesus Christ . . . crucified" (1 Cor 2:2) significant for Christian ethics and the church's response to others? It is not only significant, but it is the only thing that matters for the church to be the church.

This chapter explores the basic tenets of a theology of the cross and its related themes of suffering and salvation, revelation and authority, liberation and reconciliation, and faith and works. These are the basic theological themes that have great significance for reflecting on possible strategies for addressing global gendercide.

THE CROSS AS THEOLOGY

One cannot truly describe a theology of the cross without the danger of succumbing to another theology *about* the cross. Gerhard Forde provides a warning with his claim that "all theologies *about* the cross turn out to be theologies of glory."[2] As Christians, we often speculate about the cross's meaning, and our theologies often reduce the cross to a symbol. The cross becomes a model of suffering for the life of the Christian. In contrast, an imaginative and hope-filled theology of the cross opposes theologies that reduce the meaning of Christ's suffering to merely an example for the Christian life.

Martin Luther did not consider the cross of Christ primarily as the supreme example of humility that we are called on to imitate; instead it was that act by which Christ endured the actual punishment for our sin. "For this reason his cross is identical with ours, because he bore our punishment upon the cross."[3] As Forde says,

> The difficulty here is that the cross *is* the theo-logy, the logos of God; the word of the cross is the attack. It doesn't coin itself in ready theological propositions that we can appropriate and still go on pretty much as usual. The word of the cross kills and makes alive. It crucifies the old being in anticipation of the resurrection of the new. "The cross alone is our theology," Luther could say. And those oft-quoted words are to be taken literally. But we cannot fail to notice what an odd claim it is. How can the cross be a theology? The cross is an event. Theology is reflection on and explanation of the event. Theology is *about* the event, is it not? However, that is what makes writing some definitive theology of the cross impossible. At best all such theology can do is to clear the way for the proclamation of the cross, to drive us actually to preach the word of the cross as that folly that destroys the wisdom of the wise.[4]

---

[2]Gerhard O. Forde, *On Being a Theologian of the Cross: Reflections on Luther's Heidelberg Disputation, 1518* (Grand Rapids: Eerdmans, 1997), p. 3, emphasis original.

[3]Regin Prenter, *Luther's Theology of the Cross* (Philadelphia: Fortress, 1971), p. 3.

[4]Forde, *On Being a Theologian of the Cross*, pp. 3-4, emphasis original. Forde maintains that Luther's theology puts to rest the "optimistic appeals" of the theologian of glory by disclosing the useless efforts of persons to obtain redemption by reason, moral purity or seeking divine experiences. The suffering Christ is not a model to be imitated but rather the Savior who alone has the power to rescue sin-

The cross is not a subject for theology and speculation, but rather the center for all theology and, subsequently, Christian ethics. God works toward life and healing in hidden and mysterious ways. The work of God is surprising and unexpected. This strange manner of God, understood partially through the lens of the cross, is not merely one aspect of theology but, rather, sums up the whole of theology. It humbles a proud, triumphant church and brings that church back down firmly to the reality of the cross.

The secure grounding of the cross always brings clarity to the role of the church in its helplessness. The church is bound to this shockingly unpredictable hidden God of the cross and has no power to create except what is given through the work of the cross. Its strength, power and wisdom cannot be obtained through reason, moral duty or experience but only through the acceptance of the promise of faith (thus Paul's description of the cross as "foolishness" [1 Cor 1:18]). This acceptance can be received only in humility. For those in despair, for those oppressed and for a church centered on the cross, there is great hope! "The scene of total dereliction, of apparent weakness and folly, at Calvary is the theologian's paradigm for understanding the hidden presence and activity of God in his world and in his church."[5] The cross is the continual reminder to the church of the hidden and confounding ways of God.

Therefore, one can only describe a theology of the cross in terms of proclamation, rather than speculation. Luther's sixteenth-century description of a theology of the cross is relevant today and is helpful when

ners. Therefore, it is more precise to speak of a theologian of the cross rather than a theology of the cross.
[5]Alister E. McGrath, *Luther's Theology of the Cross* (Oxford: Blackwell, 1985), p. 181. McGrath suggests the resurgence of study of Luther and his theology of the cross in the twentieth century was a result of two devastating world wars. Nineteenth-century Protestant liberal theology was impotent when faced with overwhelming questions concerning suffering and death. Luther's theology of the cross resonated with those affected by the horror of war (pp. 179-81). He quotes Jürgen Moltmann, "Since I first studied theology, I have been concerned with the theology of the cross. . . . It is the basic theme of my theological thought. No doubt this goes back to the period of my first concern with questions concerning Christian faith and theology in real life, as a prisoner of war behind barbed wire. . . . Shattered and broken, the survivors of my generation were then returning from camps and hospitals to the lecture room. A theology which did not speak of God in terms of the abandoned and crucified one would not have got through to us then." Translated from Jürgen Moltmann, *Der gekreuzigte Gott: Das Kreuz Christi als Grund und Kritik christlicher Theologie* (Munich: Gütersloher Verlagshaus, 1981), p. 7.

considering its application to Christian ethics, and in particular the work of ending violence against women and girls. It is here in the relation between faith and ethics, between proclamation of the gospel and service to one's neighbor, that understanding often breaks down. The medieval problem of collapsing the two continues to be a perennial one that is always tempting. Luther's theology of the cross dramatically broke from this theology and practice by emphasizing the right relationship between the ultimate, faith, and the penultimate, ethics. A theology of the cross provides the foundation and direction for action in relation to the problem of violence. Although a thorough examination of what is meant by *theologia crucis* cannot be fully explored in the scope of this chapter, there are some key concepts and themes that are relevant to the application of the work to end violence.

First, it is important to fully define this theology. Luther's description in the *Heidelberg Disputation* (1518) is still relevant today.

> 18. It is certain that man must utterly despair of his own ability before he is prepared to receive the grace of Christ.

> 19. That person does not deserve to be called a theologian who looks upon the invisible things of God as though they were clearly perceptible in those things which have actually happened [Rom. 1: 20].

> 20. He deserves to be called a theologian, however, who comprehends the visible and manifest things of God seen through suffering and the cross.

> 21. A theologian of glory calls evil good and good evil. The theologian of the cross calls the thing what it actually is.[6]

Luther does not write *a* theology of the cross. Rather, he describes what those who live under the cross *do*. Luther is concerned not with the how of salvation but only that we accept by faith that the work of salvation has been completed. This theology is centered on what Christ has already accomplished through his death and resurrection. Luther's

---

[6]Martin Luther, *Luther's Works*, ed. Jaroslav Pelikan and Helmut T. Lehmann (St. Louis: Concordia, 1968), 31:39-58. *Luther's Works* cited hereafter as LW.

theology of the cross has what Forde calls "a particular perception of the world and our destiny."[7]

The cross proclaims justification by faith rather than by works. "Yes, since faith alone suffices for salvation, I need nothing except faith exercising the power and dominion of its own liberty. Lo, this is the inestimable power and liberty of Christians."[8] Therefore, works must never be the center of the Christian life. They are acts of obedience borne out of love. Good works do not make a person good, but a good person does good works. Faith in Christ frees us not from works but from false opinions concerning works.[9] This is a particularly relevant concept for considering the work of ending violence. In adopting Luther's *theologia crucis*, one must reject service to the other (the work of ending violence against women and girls) and the suffering of abused women and girls as redemptive. The pain and suffering inflicted on women is not redemptive for the victims. Rather, it is the result of sin. A theology of the cross provides an excellent lens through which to explore the proper role of suffering in human lives.

THE LANGUAGE OF THE CROSS

Language is critical for understanding the depth of the crisis and the role of the church. The cultural explanations and defenses for women undergoing genital mutilation, female infanticide, domestic violence and other atrocities crumble under the weight of the cross. The involuntary suffering endured by millions of women is not redemptive; it is a suffering borne out of opposition to a God that desires to crush such bondage. An orientation of the cross emphasizes the importance of maintaining a precise language for a Christian perspective and application. According to Gerhard Forde, our modern culture has been so sensitized and psychologized that we are afraid to call a spade a spade. We often act many times "on the assumption that our language must

---

[7]Forde, *On Being a Theologian of the Cross*, p. xii.
[8]LW 31:355.
[9]LW 31:372.

constantly be trimmed so as not to give offense, to stroke the psyche rather than to place it under attack." Our language can ultimately decline to a type of "greeting-card sentimentality."[10] Forde claims that when this happens we have lost our theological courage and legitimacy. A theology of the cross provides a paradigm or conceptual framework for a language that always speaks truth to power.

The language and meaning of the cross provide the most relevant and useful foundation for creating a practical social ethic for the work of ending violence against women and girls by identifying oppression, abuse and violence as sin, and by providing a direction and necessary focus for the church. By using the language of the cross, the church embraces the gravity of violence against women and girls. It is not a "women's issue" or merely another "social problem." It is sin that violates the integrity and humanity of God's creation. The work of Christ on the cross demands that the *whole* of the church respond to the ongoing evil and sin at work in the world. The power of God can be expressed through this language of the cross.

A theology of the cross insists on the proclamation of the gospel as the primary focus of the church. The work to end injustice is necessary, but it is not the primary work of the church. Faith and works cannot be separated, but neither should they be collapsed. There are social, economic and political realities that obstruct belief and are destructive to the integrity of humanity. The church is required to draw boundaries and declare those acts to be sinful and wrong, work to obstruct those acts, and then act in a positive manner to provide the resources for a new order. We can see examples of the church drawing those boundaries and responding to social sin throughout church history. When

---

[10]Gerhard Forde, "On Being a Theologian of the Cross," *Christian Century,* October 22, 1997, pp. 947-49, www.religion-online.org/showarticle.asp?title=320. Forde understands the danger of imprecise language resulting in the confusion of penultimate with the ultimate: "Penultimate cures are mistaken for ultimate redemption." See also Dietrich Bonhoeffer, *Ethics,* trans. Reinhard Krauss, Charles C. West and Douglas W. Stott, ed. Clifford J. Green, vol. 6 of *Dietrich Bonhoeffer Works—English Edition* (Minneapolis: Fortress, 2005), pp. 136-38. Works are necessary because Christ calls the church to act "for the other." The proclamation of the gospel is hindered where injustice exists. Evil systems and injustice obstruct belief in Jesus Christ.

some churches rejected the interference of the Nazi state in the ministry of the church, many rightly denounced the state church as the "false church." Dietrich Bonhoeffer's response and the work of the Confessing Church in Nazi Germany constitute one example, which is described in chapter five.

This aspect of the *theologia crucis*, the language of proclamation, is particularly significant for a church response to gendercide because it provides the starting point for the work. It shapes our orientation to God and others within our own historical and social context. From the perspective of the cross, violence against women is exposed as sin that divides humankind, violates the dignity of God's creation, abuses power and obstructs the gospel message of salvation and freedom.

A THEOLOGY OF REVELATION: GOD *PRO NOBIS*

A theology of the cross provides a window through which to view both God's self-revelation *and* the revelation of humankind. "The *theologia crucis,* a theology of revelation, stands in sharp contrast to speculation."[11] Through Christ's selfless act on the cross, God's nature and human nature are revealed. It is a two-edged sword that cuts through the human heart and reveals humanity's sin and need for God, and at the same time it provides salvation and healing offered by the sacrifice of Christ. Therefore, the cross is central to all of Christian theology. It is here that God and humanity are revealed in relation to each other. It is from this startling revelation that all other facets of a theology of the cross and practical applications are directed. It is because of the centrality of the cross that other theological themes on the cross are so appropriate and relevant. The gospel is always central to a theology of the cross. Everything else is built on this foundation. Sinners realize their weakness in their inability to save themselves, and through Christ's death God's love is revealed. "For Luther, the forgiveness of sins means more than a doctrine to be believed" and more than a merely subjective experience. It is a genuine act of the merciful God, through the living Christ, by which

---

[11]McGrath, *Luther's Theology of the Cross,* p. 149.

God, in unconditional, unmerited love, establishes relationship with a sinful humanity.[12]

From this perspective, a theology of the cross provides the critical direction for the mission of the church. Without an understanding of the central role of the cross and its message, Christians are in danger of placing ethics at the center of their theology or dismissing works altogether as nonessential for living a life of faith. More importantly, works ultimately can become a form of idolatry without an understanding of the cross. A theology of glory replaces a theology of the cross, dismissing the power of the death and resurrection of Christ. This dualism is a perennial problem in the history of the Christian church and is heightened in the American church today. The American ideals of independence and individualism have shaped some churches' views to such an extent that care for the poor and marginalized is thought to be too politically radical. The same values shape other churches to such an extent that social change efforts have shifted from being a penultimate work to the ultimate focus. The resurrection is preached without the cross. Both theological interpretations have lost their will to speak truth to power. The power to create real change is lost in relationship to the church's move away from the theology of the cross.

The ontological questions of the identity of God and persons must be central. They are answered by the saving act on the cross. The hidden God is revealed only through suffering and the cross. It is here that humanity's true nature is exposed and subsequently redeemed. This can best be understood when viewed in their relation to each other. God can be known not in the abstract but only in relation to each person. The living and dynamic act of Christ on the cross is personal and effectual.[13] God is the transcendent and the incarnate justifier. The divine essence of God cannot be separated from God's will and mission. Ontology shapes function.

---

[12]Philip S. Watson, *Let God Be God! An Interpretation of the Theology of Martin Luther* (London: Epworth Press, 1947), p. 27.

[13]Ibid., p. 24.

The cornerstone of a theology of the cross is the fact that we are justified by faith. The early medieval understanding of "the righteousness of God" as one's struggle to achieve righteousness had led to years of struggle for Martin Luther. All his good works, including fasting, prayers and self-deprivations, only led him to despair. Staupitz, Luther's mentor, helped Luther struggle through his *Anfechtungen* (afflictions) by leading him to look to the wounds of Christ on the cross. It was while meditating on Romans 1:17 that "the righteousness of God" took on new meaning. Here Luther understood God's righteousness as passive righteousness, that is, as a gift not a demand. There was nothing that one could do to merit salvation. God's gift of righteousness justifies the sinner before God. The message of the cross is the paradoxical message of freedom as bondage to Christ. The new understanding of God's righteousness helped Luther to distinguish between law and gospel.[14] God's right-eousness was not condemnation but grace that justifies and saves sinners. This radical new understanding of righteousness as gift freed Luther from anxiety about salvation and from the accompanying effort of striving for salvation. This was to become central to Luther's develop-ment of every other aspect of his theology. For example, the role of works changes from being a requirement for salvation to an expression of the love of God. Love is no longer seen as focused on our love toward God expressed through acts of merit but rather as God's love toward us. In this new understanding Luther became aware of a radically different God from the one whom he had feared and hated.[15] He now under-stood God to be merciful, full of love and grace. More powerfully, this insight was much deeper than a new abstract conception of God. Luther entered into a relationship with God based on an acceptance of God's committed love for him. All works and penances added nothing toward the gift and promise of this ultimate love and gift of God.

Luther now realized that God was revealed in a powerful way through Christ on the cross. At the moment of Christ's death the temple curtain

---

[14]LW 34:336-37.
[15]Watson, *Let God Be God!*, p. 20.

was torn apart. It was now possible to enter into the holy of holies, that is, into relationship with God. The law is necessary to create order but does not calm the anxieties of the godly that fear judgment. Only the gospel provides the "good news" that God entered into the world in a real, concrete way. Liberation is only possible by Christ's giving of himself. It is only through Christ, not the law, that one is saved. This saving moment tears the curtain between God and humankind and allows believers to enter into union with God through the Christ of the cross.

For Luther, this new perception of God changed everything. The incarnate Christ was now understood to be a loving Savior who sacrificed himself in order that sins might be forgiven and new life be given to sinners. In realizing that Christ's own righteousness captures human sin, Luther began to understand the nature of God. God is not only judge but lover. Luther's entire paradigm of the relationship between faith and ethics shattered. The tired medieval schema of works righteousness lost all power to persuade and was replaced by the life-giving release of God's freedom and Spirit. The meaning of the law changed for Luther and those who accepted this theology of the cross. The law was no longer seen as a set of conditions to work through for salvation. The law viewed through the lens of the cross was recognized as the rock against which humanity's sin and pride were broken. Subsequently, the faithful are driven to the foot of the cross in humility. The surrender of human pride and self-interest allows for the acceptance of Christ's forgiveness, grace and life. Luther argued that works righteousness minimized the work that Christ had already accomplished on the cross. He wrote from his own experience of the agony and futility of working for acceptance and redemption. Therefore, from this perspective ethics and the mission of the church begin at the cross.

Luther expressed his conviction that Christ's incarnation and saving work not only revealed Christ's *agape* love but reflected God's deep concern and love for his people. In focusing on the hidden God of majesty and might, one was in danger of becoming terrified and fearful of a judging God. Luther exhorted his readers to view God as a loving

God who sacrificed his only Son so that believers could enter into a life of freedom from fear. The divine is found in the self-giving love of Christ. God was no longer a distant, cold and judgmental being needing to be placated with indulgences and fasting. Condemnation had been lifted for believers. Luther provides a reminder to Christians today that Christ was given "from a motive of pure love."[16] A refusal to trust in God's promise is to diminish Christ's work of salvation. In "Sermons on the Gospel of St. John Chapters 1–4," Luther used biblical language to express the new relationship that is given to believers in Christ. Like a loving parent God draws each one close like chicks to a mother hen. Recognizing both the powerful feminine imagery and the masculine imagery of God shatters the view of God as an avenging God in need of humanity's sacrifices and works in order to provide intimacy and salvation. According to Luther, in keeping with biblical theology, nothing else is needed for salvation. God's love was powerfully manifested by the death of Jesus on the cross. To think one can add to the work of the cross is pure folly.

Luther distinguishes between the two works of God: alien and proper. His understanding of these two works helps to clarify and define the roles of both God and humanity in the death and resurrection of Jesus. For it is here that humanity's wretched condition and God's "pure love" interface. The power of this saving event is so cataclysmic that the believer's relationship with God is changed for all time. Both these works of God in the cross and resurrection renew the original relationship of God to humanity. It is a relationship marked with love and intimacy. However, the nature of this intimacy with God is known only in a "hidden" way. The majesty and glory of the "face of God" is never exposed and can never be known. For God is only partially known through the faith of the believer. "The 'friends of the cross' know that beneath the humility and shame of the cross lie concealed the power and the glory of God—but to others, this insight is denied."[17] What is

---

[16]LW 22:374.
[17]McGrath, *Luther's Theology of the Cross,* pp. 149-50.

made known to us through Christ as true revelation is also concealed
and indirect. The revelation of God through the cross is an indirect revelation. There is a paradox found at the foot of the cross. God is both
known and hidden in that revelation.[18]

The revealed God (*deus revelatus*) is set against the hidden God (*deus
absconditus*). Luther made the distinctions with confidence because "he
knew that no one—no earthly theologian certainly—was going to dis-
lodge, spy out, or unmask the naked, hidden God. The naked, hidden
God needs no theological proof, apology, or defense."[19] In Christ, God
is hidden in suffering and God is revealed through the suffering Christ;
in this way the believer shares in the life of Christ by taking up his or her
own cross. This does not occur in an imitative manner as if suffering
would somehow restore salvation. Rather, it is always in the context of
our relationship to Christ. The Christian enters suffering and there finds
Christ. This confounding God acts and reveals himself *sub contraria
specie,* under the appearance of the opposite, in the Christ who is hidden
in suffering. The church and Christian life, therefore, also are found in
the midst of suffering. God's strength is found in weakness, life is borne
from death and grace is given through his judgment. Through suffering
and the cross, Christ and life are found. Through this violent act the
greatest love erupts in the very being of Christ. Luther's fixation on the
centrality of the cross, that is, the centrality of the revelation of God,
provides the foundation for ethics and social justice. Humankind looks
for God in the powerful manifestations of the world and finds only
empty glory. As Christ was born in the hiddenness of poverty and
weakness, so he dies in suffering on the cross. The power and glory of
God are hidden behind the unexpected cradle and cross. The ethical
implications are profound. The God we follow is found only through

---

[18]Ibid., p. 149.

[19]Gerhard O. Forde, *Theology Is for Proclamation* (Minneapolis: Fortress, 1990), p. 22. Accordingly,
Luther saw the problem not as finding God but rather as "getting God off our backs." Since only God
is able to do that, God deals with God. According to Forde, since we are "inveterate theologians of
glory," God's revelation must take place *sub contrario,* under the form of opposition. See Forde, *On
Being a Theologian of the Cross,* p. 31.

faith. The church of Christ, therefore, is called to live out its mission among the suffering and weak, the unexpected spaces and places in the world.

THE MEANING AND ROLE OF SUFFERING

Suffering, whether voluntary or involuntary, is the context in which we live our lives. However, within this reality of suffering we can be assured that God meets us in our powerlessness and weakness. This is a great message of hope to abused women and girls. Nevertheless, it is a great challenge to the church to be Christ for the suffering and oppressed. The work to end suffering and at the same time be present with the suffering is the tension the church must live within. The church is humbled at the foot of the cross, identifies with those suffering and takes up the cross. Paradoxically, by engaging in this work of Christ, in the shadow of death and pain, life is found.

A perspective of the cross addresses the perennial theological question of theodicy. How does a God of love allow the cruel reality of oppression and tyranny that causes the suffering of millions of women and girls worldwide? How does an all-powerful God refrain from crushing evil systems of injustice? The perspective of the cross provides an answer. God does not prevent humanity from acting according to its nature. However, through the cross evil is ultimately conquered. The will of God is always toward love and life. Christ is there in the place of the suffering and weakness of the oppressed and is present, not in the abstract, but in the present reality of the world.

This power of God is ultimate and is always working creatively through the penultimate confines of our cultural and political context. What does this mean for Christians? The call for all Christians is to enter into this creative work of God and participate in the life-giving activity of peacemaking and justice building. Christian ethics and, more narrowly, social justice do not have any particular power to solve the problems associated with violence. The power to overcome evil and violence is rooted in God's love alone. From this foundation, manifest through the revelation of Jesus Christ, power and grace are available to those who dare to enter into this difficult mission. The work of justice making costs the followers of Jesus. What is required of a radical disciple and the authentic church of Christ is a willingness to abandon an agenda often marked by self-preservation and pride. A church concerned with the promotion of narrow political ideologies, the advancement of church growth and the creation of a comfortable space has forgotten the mission of the gospel and Bonhoeffer's "cost of discipleship." Entering into the powerful, creative work of Christ means a commitment to work in service to others in detachment from self-regard and self-preservation. Suffering is the context in which we live and, paradoxically, the burden we are called to lift from others' lives.

However, instruction regarding the reality of suffering in Christians' lives has also been used as an ideological tool to maintain power over women's and girls' lives. Too many times abused women have reported that teaching and counsel on the subject of suffering have led them to remain in abusive homes. They have been told that their suffering should be "offered up to God" and that suffering will "build up" their character. This is a horrific perversion of the teaching of the cross. The pain inflicted on women and girls is not salvific and does not make one holy. This type of suffering is a result of the oppressor's sin and cultural and religious supports for the denigration and abuse of women and girls. The teaching of the theology of the cross counters the idea that oppression and abuse are in any way redemptive. Only Christ's voluntary sacrifice on the cross and the power of his resurrection are redemptive. Women and girls' suffering results from evil, not good. I have witnessed the freedom that women and girls begin to experience when they realize the teaching they have received on suffering is oppressive and should be replaced by the good news that they don't need to suffer for Christ in these debilitating ways. The good news of the cross is that Christ has already freed them from having to endure this type of suffering. Christ knows their pain and is present with them in all their suffering. God is truly *for them.*

THE DIALECTIC OF FAITH AND WORKS

One of Luther's central theological themes is freedom. In the one event of the cross believers are justified and thereby live out the call of God. This is a call to freedom. This cornerstone of a theology of the cross is the foundation for Christian ethics. It is from this point of departure that one can rightly discuss the place of works.

Luther's *theologia crucis* provides the framework for an understanding of the relationship between faith and works. More specifically, Luther's theology completely alters the relationship between faith and ethics. From this perspective, ethics is the necessary response to grace; works flow from faith. For the Christian, it is faith that provides the power to serve his or her neighbor. A summary discussion of the relationship of faith and works is needed to provide a context for arguing for the church's responsibility for responding to the problem of violence against women in a comprehensive manner.[20] This dialectical relationship is helpful in countering the contemporary church's tendency to either collapse or separate faith and works, that is, confuse the relationship of one to the other.

The proper role of works is better understood from a perspective rooted in a theology of the cross. Works can then be understood as a response of gratitude to God's great love. One becomes freed from self-expectation and legal requirements. Therefore, through justification the Christian is able to work in community toward solutions to the world's problems. There is no fanciful delusion that a Christian kingdom can be established here. Nevertheless, the work is done with great hope in the

---

[20]Faith as the foundation for ethics in Luther's theology of the cross is the theme of ongoing research. See for example: Lindberg, *Beyond Charity*; idem, "Luther's Concept of Offering," *Dialog* 35 (Fall 1996): 251-57; idem, "Do Lutherans Shout Justification but Whisper Sanctification?" *Lutheran Quarterly* 13 (1999): 1-20; idem, "Theory and Practice: Reformation Models of Ministry as Resource for the Present," *Lutheran Quarterly* 27 (1975): 27-35; George W. Forell, *Faith Active in Love: An Investigation of the Principles Underlying Luther's Social Ethics* (New York: American Press, 1954); idem, *The Christian Lifestyle: Reflections on Romans 12–15* (Philadelphia: Fortress, 1975); idem, *The Proclamation of the Gospel in a Pluralistic World: Essays on Christianity and Culture* (Philadelphia: Fortress, 1973); Gerhard O. Forde, *Theology Is for Proclamation*; idem, *On Being A Theologian of the Cross*; Heinrich Bornkamm, *Luther's Doctrine of the Two Kingdoms in the Context of His Theology*, trans. (Philadelphia: Fortress, 1966); Gerhard Ebeling, *Luther: An Introduction to His Thought*, trans. R. A. Wilson (Philadelphia: Fortress, 1970); Gerta Scharffenorth, *Becoming Friends in Christ: The Relationship Between Man and Woman as Seen by Luther* (Geneva: Lutheran World Federation, 1983).

realization that Christ gives grace and power to bring healing, comfort and freedom to those who are oppressed and suffering. The Christian is freed from the burden of seeking his or her own salvation in service. One need only care for the other using the knowledge, resources and support available. Therefore, justification and ethics are connected at the cross.

There is a radical change that happens outside of ourselves (*extra nos*) because of the death and resurrection of Jesus. Believers' lives are not just improved but altered completely. The relationship between God and humanity is different, something new. Believers remain sinners but are made righteous by Christ's work (*simul iustus et peccator*). Christians enter into a new intimacy with God that is marked by freedom and joy. Service is freely given out of obedience and gratitude. The Christian is raised up in Christ. The result of Christ's sacrifice is freedom for the sinner from the effects of sin and death. One's very identity changes as a result of the work of Christ. It is faith that empowers works. Without faith, works are dead in relation to salvation. Therefore, apart from faith, works lack the power to transform the person and bring about reconciliation between God and the person. According to Luther, if faith is not central, then the entire gospel is lost.

True liberation finds its source only in the power that is rooted in God alone. The danger in operating from a theology of ethics is the possible consequential self-delusion that only one type of Christian solution must be employed. This type of social gospel inevitably leads to disappointment. Christian history is filled with examples of Christians attempting to Christianize society in order to eradicate evil deeds. These attempts ultimately lead to tyranny and persecution. The apparent good of social justice can become another form of idolatry. Understanding the dialectical relationship of faith and ethics within a perspective of a theology of the cross underscores the primary gift of faith given by God alone and the offering of that love within a cultural context to further justice and freedom. Ethics and service to others are the reflection and effect of God's power rooted in faith. In this way confidence and trust in God replace religious zealotry and political ideologies.

Therefore, based on God's love *pro nobis,* the Christian responds by love for the other. This freedom creates a transforming love because it is rooted in God's power. Service to one's neighbor in this context alone is favorable to God. God's power in contrast to worldly power always leads to freedom, and this power is always a spiritual power[21] capable of crushing the terror of violence and oppression. God's grace also frees us to act for the other. Luther sums up his dialectic of "freedom and bondage of the spirit" in the following passage:

> A Christian is a perfectly free lord of all, subject to none.
> A Christian is a perfectly dutiful servant of all, subject to all.
> These two theses seem to contradict each other. If, however, they should be found to fit together they would serve our purpose beautifully. Both are Paul's own statements, who says in I Cor. 9[:19], "For though I am free from all men, I have made myself a slave to all," and in Rom. 13[:8], "Owe no one anything, except to love one another." Love by its very nature is ready to serve and be subject to him who is loved. So Christ, although he was Lord of all, was "born of woman, born under the law" [Gal. 4:4], and therefore was at the same time a free man and a servant, "in the form of God" and "of a servant" [Phil. 2:6-8].[22]

Carter Lindberg argued that Luther related social ethics to the doctrine of justification within this one passage from *Freedom of a Christian.*[23] God's kingdom is a realm marked by peace, reconciliation and grace. The disciple is truly free in Christ and therefore bound to serve his or her neighbor. The community of believers, knowing that they serve not by striving toward perfection but rather by working in the "real world," is not afraid to join with others of different belief systems in order to extend peace and reconciliation to others. Holiness is not characterized by personal piety and social perfection but by the courage to live out one's fullness of humanity in obedience to Christ.

Service given to one's neighbor as a result of faith is free because

---

[21]LW 31:335.

[22]LW 31:344.

[23]Lindberg, *Beyond Charity,* p. 99. Lindberg notes that in this passage Luther "succinctly related the social ethics of the Reformation to his doctrine of justification."

there is no expectation that any works are redemptive. Therefore, social ethics is not dependent on its results. There is an intrinsic value in the neighbor. There is no merit gained in love; it is a free gift. Love is directed toward one's neighbor, not only in obedience to Christ's command to serve but because Christ lives in one's neighbor. Justification by faith frees the church to direct its focus away from itself and its very survival to care for others. This love is disinterested. It is for the sake of others alone that we serve, not for our own salvation or any other personal or political gain. Proclamation of the gospel cannot be divorced from the love of neighbor. Jesus' proclamation of the first two commandments is always related and they cannot be separated from each other.

Responsibility toward the neighbor extends beyond individual service. Christians are responsible to act in order to bring about justice in the social and also the political arenas. The demand to care for one's neighbor broadens ethics to a larger arena beyond personal morality. The church needs to be involved in the area of politics. This is controversial, and critics would argue that the Christian church should have nothing to do with worldly affairs. Nevertheless, the church should move beyond self-protection and personal morality and work in the arena of Christ, here among its neighbors. It is in the world that the church finds the suffering and oppressed and so finds Christ at work. To abandon the call to root out evil systems that support violence is to abandon Christ's mission.

Luther's perspective on faith and works also serves to reject viewing "rights" and "liberties" as abstractions; rather, they are concrete realities that Christians are called to promote for the improvement of humanity.[24] As a result of faith in God alone, Christians are free to serve in the political and social realm without insisting on the establishment of a Christian kingdom on earth. It is the sin of idolatry to maintain that power is a result of one's superior race, gender, political affiliation or government. Power is spiritual, and it operates through believers' works

---

[24]Forell, *Proclamation of the Gospel,* pp. 128-29.

by way of faith in Christ, who is the source of all power. Jesus rejected Satan's enticement to seize power apart from God. Freedom and power for the Christian have their source in God alone.

> Christian freedom releases men from bondage to all political mythologies and other absolute loyalties. . . . The relation of Christian freedom to other liberties and rights is similar to its relation to religious liberty. Man is unwilling to grant rights to others because of his idolization of the principalities and powers whose rule these liberties threaten. It is because of the idolization of my "race" that the freedoms of other races are reduced. It is because of the threat to my group's political and economic idols that the freedom of those who oppose them is abrogated. And the uncritical and idolatrous deification of my religious institutions makes me demand the suppression or even extermination of all religious institutions which differ from my own. Christian freedom, by releasing man from all false gods, obviates the necessity of defending these idols at the cost of the rights and liberties of other men. Since salvation is not racial, national, political, economic, or even "religious," the ultimate devotion to these causes is unmasked as idolatrous worship of false gods, and man is freed from idolatry for the service of the person of the neighbor. He is freed from serving the "Sabbath" to serving man.[25]

The ideology that promotes work for just causes as a means to salvation or for the purpose of establishing a Christian kingdom on earth is in danger of being reduced to a form of idol worship. In keeping faith in a primary role, and works in a necessary but secondary role, the believer is relieved of anxiety for the future and the fear of death. Consequently, salvation remains in Christ rather than in any good works, including justice work. Service is freely given in obedience to God.

Luther's doctrine of the two kingdoms was not a framework for understanding the divine and secular realms as two separate arenas whereby Christians are called to participate only in those activities that are defined as being of the supernatural realm.[26] Luther was concerned

---

[25]Ibid., pp. 32-33.
[26]See Lindberg, *Beyond Charity,* pp. 161-62, for a summary description of the widely held but erroneous theological viewpoint that Luther was a quietist and disinterested in worldly affairs.

with the person's relation to the world from a perspective of faith. According to Luther, there is a distinction between the two kingdoms, but there is never a complete separation. Problems arise when believers ignore that distinction and attempt to build a heavenly kingdom on earth—or separate the two kingdoms in such a way that the earthly is held in contempt and ignored.

Several years ago, while acting in my role as director of a battered women's program, I attempted to contact all the churches in our small city with a Christmas request. I hoped that each church would "adopt" a family. This would involve receiving a list of the ages and genders of the children and women residing in the safe shelter and providing Christmas gifts for them and perhaps some financial assistance in starting their new lives. It was rewarding for both the families and the churches who did participate, but it was also sad to hear the comments from pastors who refused to participate. The most common comment offered was in reference to the shelter being "secular" and not Christian in identity. They did not want to support a "feminist" or secular organization. Each woman and child did receive gifts that year. However, how sad for the churches who missed Christ in those women and children. For these pastors their "two kingdoms" were so separated that they held a detached confessionalism that limited their mission to preaching the Word without serving their "unworthy" neighbor. They failed to grasp the incarnational nature of the cross of Christ that extends mission to all people. Christ's kingdom is not defined by penultimate ideologies, but neither can it be separated from the world he entered and loved. A theology of the cross and resurrection provides a framework for supporting the dialectical relation between the two kingdoms. The kingdom of God is in the here and now and in the encounter with the suffering of the marginalized, oppressed and abused. Ethics rests upon the dynamic, living and unchanging relationship of God to the world and God's ultimate power to create change in this temporary, penultimate world through the church community.

THE CONTEXT FOR MISSION: THE COMMUNITY

It is one of my arguments that the whole of the church must respond to the problem of gendercide as a social, political and human rights problem. It is the responsibility of the Christian church to address evil from the standpoint of a worshiping community. Violence against women and girls is primarily a theological issue because it perverts human relationships and devalues the dignity of the person. In defining the problem in this manner the church as a whole must denounce the violence, take steps to aid the victims, and have a clear plan to hold accountable secular and church institutions that collude with culpable governmental and criminal justice systems. A theology of the cross, in which the dialectic of faith and works is central, provides a foundation for challenging the church in this role. It is the proclamation of the gospel that the church receives the transforming power to change lives and social systems. Lindberg illustrates this perspective in his discussion of the application of Luther's theology to social welfare. He argues that Luther maintains that the church is the instrument through which God works to address evil in the world. "Luther had the boldness to address structural sources of injustice and to advocate legislative redress of them because his social ethics was rooted in the worship and proclamation of the community. The congregation is the local source in which God 'creates a new world.'" Luther's concern for social welfare was a significant shift from medieval piety to social ethics.[27] Lindberg notes that, for Luther, *Gottesdienst* (translated typically as "worship") means "God's service." Worship is the root and context in which we are able to serve. Therefore, love for the neighbor is rooted in the creative love of God that we encounter in worship.

> Luther does not speak of social ethics per se, but that does not mean that in our sense of the phrase he did not develop it. What Luther does speak

---

[27]Ibid., p. 163. Lindberg refers to Luther's treatises "The Blessed Sacrament of the Holy and True Body of Christ and the Brotherhoods" (1519) and "To the Christian Nobility of the German Nation" (1520) to illustrate Luther's attack on the medieval institutions that promulgated rampant efforts at achievement piety.

of is service to the neighbor, service that is inseparable from service to
God—indeed, is service to God. . . . It is because God serves us that we
serve others. As Vilmos Vajta has emphasized in his thorough study of
Luther's theology of worship, worship and service to others are inseparable. There is no doubt then that both worship and service are corporate and communal. . . . The reform of worship included the renewal
of social life. . . . "Now there is no greater service of God [*gottis dienst*]
than Christian love which helps and serves the needy" (LW 45:172 . . .).
Worship creates the community and the community serves others. The
work of the people does not stop at worship but rather begins there as
the work of the people for the benefit of others—in what has been called
"the liturgy after the liturgy."[28]

Luther considers the daily work of the Christian to be worship because
it embodies obedience to God's will. Worship within the community is
at the heart of all Christian work.

These efforts do not derive from the believers' own acting love but
rather are a result of God's love flowing through Christians. Ethics
emerges from the faith of the worshiping community. "Only faith [can]
guarantee ethical action."[29] Luther rejected individualistic philosophical
ethics since this view asserts that human works are necessary for one's
happiness. In medieval theology, self-denial was an important factor in
achieving a piety that unites with grace to attain the ultimate good. According to Luther, the emphasis on human effort needed to be shifted
to God's work already achieved in Christ. There was a place for philosophy, and certainly reason, but the problem surfaced when philosophy entered the realm of theology. The focus on human effort undermined the centrality of justification by faith.[30] An ethic of the cross

---

[28]Ibid., pp. 163-64.

[29]Forell, *Faith Active in Love?*, p. 79.

[30]Ibid., pp. 79-81. See pp. 79-84 for a full discussion of Luther's opinion of Aristotle, scholasticism and
the influence of Greek philosophy on theology. See also Timothy George, *Theology of the Reformers*
(Nashville: Broadman, 1988), pp. 51-79, for a more detailed analysis of Luther's theological development. Forell summarized Luther's view on Aristotle: "Luther had nothing against Aristotle as such.
What he rejected was the whole effort in scholastic theology to make Aristotelian philosophy the
presupposition of Christian doctrine, to interpret biblical revelation in terms of pagan 'sophistry,' to
reduce the great themes of Scripture, grace, faith, justification, to scholastic jargon. In the spirit of

is based on God's revelation and therefore is personal. The church's social ethic originates from grace received through Christ. The gospel issues the command to be for the other as God is *pro nobis*. Therefore, justification is the basis for all Christian ethics.[31]

It is faith that provides the power and hope for good works. The righteousness bestowed on the believer as a godly gift enables a thirst for justice and love to be extended to the neighbor. Both exist together, but faith gives shape and power to the work of serving others.[32] Luther's Christology shines through in his discussion of ethics. Christ saves and then empowers the church to serve in the world. The purpose of all service is to glorify God. Within Luther's understanding of a theology of the cross, the medieval anthropocentric ethics dramatically shift. What Luther considers true Christianity is uncovered: Christ alone saves and transforms. In our worship we care for our neighbor as an act of love. It is in this way that Christians glorify God.[33]

The sacrament of communion shared together as a body reveals the basic principles of Christian life together. Faith is received and love activated by the Spirit. These two principles are inextricably linked together within the context of the worshiping body. Faith is personal, and love is concretely demonstrated within the body. The relationship in the presence of God (*coram Deo*) always shows the way to one's relationship before the neighbor (*coram hominibus*). This intimate union of faith and love becomes an ethic of the first commandment. As the cross is the sacred place where faith and ethics unite, so it is that faith received and love demonstrated within and outside the worshiping community contain the whole of the Christian doctrine.

Luther's perspective on faith and works is one key to understanding the theology of the cross. Faith without works is dead, and works without faith are idolatry. The center of Christian life is the worship of

---

Tertullian, Luther asked what Jerusalem had to do with Athens, the Church with the Academy, faith with reason" (Forell: *Faith Active in Love?*, pp. 57-58).

[31]Forell, *Faith Active in Love?*, pp. 83-84.

[32]LW 26:133.

[33]LW 26:449.

God through the proclamation of the gospel and service to neighbor. The source of all faith and thereby works is Christ. To believe and trust in the saving grace of God is also to receive the power authentically to address evil in the world. Works of love apart from faith often lead to a false ethical idealism. Love flowing from faith is powerful, spontaneous and realistic. Luther understood the danger of confusing the roles of faith and love. He had personally suffered through the torment of self-analysis and self-denial in attempting to achieve a righteousness acceptable to God. Luther obtained spiritual freedom when he accepted the biblical message of justification by *sola fides* (faith alone). His condemnation of medieval scholasticism in the strongest possible language was a result of seeing the effects of a works-righteousness theology on the church. The egocentrism of medieval anthropological theology was concerned with the improvement of the self rather the good of the neighbor. Luther's *theologia crucis* places Christ as central and challenges the worshiping community to proclaim the gospel through selfless service.

This Reformation theology has great relevance to our contemporary church situation. The perennial problem of either embracing works as a means of salvation or ignoring justice making as a critical and necessary work for the church continues to have a negative impact on the church as some churches struggle to shape their understanding of the relationship of faith and mission. However, a recovery of a theology of the cross as a foundation for creating hopeful, imaginative and powerful responses to care for the neighbor is embraced by some, and offers creative possibilities for addressing violence and other social problems.

CONCLUSION

All these important theological themes of the cross—relation of faith and works, the role of suffering, communal worship as the foundation for ethics and understanding the revelation of God hidden but fully realized in Christ's death and resurrection—are powerful realities for moving the Christian church to a holistic and hopeful force for creating positive change in the lives of millions of women and girls around the world. The power of the cross crushes the idolatry of power that leads to the denigration of women and girls and crushes the ideologies that keep women and girls from realizing their full potential as human beings with dignity. The language of the cross is freedom and promise that has real meaning for working to end systems that enslave mind-numbing numbers of women and children.

A theology of the cross and resurrection bridges the chasm between Christ and humanity. The outpouring of the Holy Spirit on the church enables the church to do the works desired by God, that is, bring healing, peace and reconciliation to a broken world. Theology of the cross also includes the message of freedom to those enslaved by abuse, oppression and violence. This intimate partnership between Christ and the followers of Christ enables disciples to be prophets of peace and workers of justice. This gospel teaching, and Reformation reminder, of the significance of the cross clarifies the meaning of this work: it is not for salvation; it is not to attain holiness or gain self-improvement. It is the mission of God's followers to embrace others (not in the abstract but in reality) as a result of the grace and forgiveness given to them.

A characteristic of this relationship with God is its hidden nature. We recognize Christ and Christ's mission not in the obvious and spectacular. Christ is in the poor, the marginalized, the suffering of the world. Jesus persists in this message (Mt 25:34-40). Accounts of Jesus' concern for the rejected, his defense of the persecuted and his disregard for social norms that demeaned the foreigner, women and the shamed are not merely moral stories. Through his relationship with the marginalized and oppressed, he revealed the nature of God and the mission of God. Jesus' entrance into the world as a poor baby born in a poor occupied country was no accident. Rather than entering as a royal king demanding allegiance (this would be most reasonable), he entered quietly and without the world's recognition, save for a few. What meaning does this have for the church today? Through the perspective of a theology of the cross and resurrection, the church comes to understand that the God we worship is a God who can be found only at the foot of the cross and only by way of faith. It is only through faith in the promises rooted in grace that one can follow Christ in the work of reconciliation and establishing justice. The work to end violence against women and girls *is* the ongoing working of God's love in the world. This work does not offer salvation for the disciple; rather, it is a work rooted in communal worship that offers participation in the life and work of Christ.

5

DIETRICH BONHOEFFER'S CONFESSION AND RESISTANCE

A Model for a Church Response to Gendercide

The church confesses that it has not professed openly and clearly enough its message of the one God, revealed for all times in Jesus Christ and tolerating no other gods besides. The church confesses its timidity, itsdeviations, its dangerous concessions. It has often disavowed its duties [Ämter] as sentinel and comforter. Through this it has often withheld the compassion that it owes to the despised and rejected. The church was mute when it should have cried out, because the blood of the innocent cried out to heaven. The church did not find the right word in the right way at the right time.

DIETRICH BONHOEFFER

INTRODUCTION

Violence against women violates human dignity in numerous forms and on many levels. I have defined violence against women and girls in both the theological language of sin and in legal language as a crime and violation of human rights. It is my purpose to call a spade a spade by identifying gender violence in the strongest possible language in order to emphasize the gravity of the problem and, consequently, the need for the church to address the problem in a holistic manner. Internationally, millions of women have been denigrated by rape, torture, physical battering, and psychological and economic oppression. Gendercide is a type of holocaust that demands the response of the *whole* of the church. Therefore, it is helpful to reflect on a contemporary historical event that brought the church to a place of crisis and demanded of the church a response to horrific injustice and the systematic torture and death of millions. Dietrich Bonhoeffer (1906–1945) and the Confessing Church's response to the evil propaganda and deeds of the Nazi state provide a helpful example of one church response that was rooted in a theology of the cross.

Bonhoeffer also provides a contemporary interpretation of an ethic of resistance to institutions that systematically promoted racism and ultimately death. His confession and activism offer a profound example of the impact of deliberate discipleship and the power of community to effect change. These are important lessons for the church when considering a thoughtful and active response to violence against women and girls. Dietrich Bonhoeffer's response to an oppressive government that interfered with the rights of its people was rooted in his theology of the cross. He understood the significance of the cross and Christ's vicarious representative action as the place where faith and ethics meet. Humanity is drawn into the reality of God's ability to continually create anew. The work of peace and reconciliation in the world is shaped by God's will to always be moving toward life and the fullness of love. This is the power, joy and hope of the cross and resurrection in a world fractured by violence. Human reason cannot perceive the way of God. It is only through the crucified one that the church perceives the will of God and God's mission. Service and love imagined and realized in Christ manifest the creative power for social and structural change.

Dietrich Bonhoeffer: His Practical Application of Luther's *Theologia Crucis*

There are several reasons for including reflections on Dietrich Bonhoeffer's theology, ethics and activism when considering possible church responses to violence against women and girls. First, Bonhoeffer provides a valuable, contemporary example of the methodology and consequences of applying a theology of the cross to the problem of institutionalized evil. Second, Bonhoeffer offers a model of a practical application of a theology that roots ethics in proclamation. Bonhoeffer's Christology is the starting point for his commitment to social and political justice. Christ and the human relationship *coram Deo* and *coram hominibus* inform Bonhoeffer's life and work. His central proclamation of the suffering Christ allowed him to identify with the oppressed and challenge the church to advocate with all who suffer. Third, Bonhoeffer remained within his denominational confession and relied on his Reformation theological stance to justify his resistance work against National Socialism and the German Christians. Bonhoeffer argued for the church's responsibility to move beyond confession to resistance when faced with a situation of *status confessionis*.[1] His work informed the later ecumenical church stance against South African apartheid, which argued that racism is a confessional matter. A study of Bonhoeffer's practical application of Luther's theology of the cross can act as a guide when considering what role the church should take concerning violence against women. Fourth, Bonhoeffer and the Confessing Church provide lessons concerning issues of church unity, identity and obedience to the gospel in the face of condemnation that can be applied directly to the current problem of violence against women and girls. The confession of the gospel led to their active resistance to that evil. The discussion and analysis of the relationship of confession and resistance (faith and works) as it relates to the theology and activism of Dietrich Bonhoeffer are relevant in framing a theological response to global violence against women and girls.

ETHICS: FREEDOM AND RESPONSIBILITY

Dietrich Bonhoeffer maintained that Christ is the point of departure for

---

[1]Eberhard Bethge, *Friendship and Resistance: Essays on Dietrich Bonhoeffer* (Grand Rapids: Eerdmans, 1995), p. 27.

ethics for the Christian church. Therefore, questions regarding the good
and what must be done are not relevant as starting points for Christian
ethics. Bonhoeffer, deeply rooted in Luther's theology of the cross,
argued that it is the character of God found in the revelation of Christ
that shapes the most relevant ethical question, "What is the will of
God?" This radical center of Christian ethics reveals the assumption
about ultimate reality.

> When the ethical problem presents itself essentially as the question of
> my own being good and doing good, the decision has already been made
> that the self and the world are the ultimate realities. All ethical reflection
> then has the goal that I be good, and that the world—by my action—be-
> comes good. If it turns out, however, that these realities, myself and the
> world, are themselves embedded in a wholly other ultimate reality,
> namely, the reality of God the Creator, Reconciler, and Redeemer, then
> the ethical problem takes on a whole new aspect. Of ultimate impor-
> tance, then, is not that I become good, or that the condition of the world
> be improved by my efforts, but that the reality of God show itself every-
> where to be the ultimate reality.[2]

This description of the meaning and center of Christian ethics shapes
Bonhoeffer's understanding of how the church must respond to the
atrocities resulting from the Nazi regime. All theological and ethical
reflection begins in prayer, discernment and understanding of the will
of God, who is the world's ultimate reality. God's concern and work in
the world take place through the church community concretely and
realistically. If this radical ethic is embraced by the church, then the
focus moves away from the common understanding of ethics as being
good and doing good to the reality of the God we know within the
context of our time and place. This incarnational embrace of christocentric ethics helps to continually guide the church into entering the
ongoing work of Christ in the world. For Bonhoeffer, there is only

---

[2]Dietrich Bonhoeffer, *Ethics*, trans. Reinhard Krauss, Charles C. West and Douglas W. Stott, ed. Clifford J. Green, vol. 6 of *Dietrich Bonhoeffer Works—English Edition* (Minneapolis: Fortress, 2005), pp.
47-58.

one reality. That reality is "Christ as center" for both the church and the world.

> What matters is *participating in the reality of God and the world in Jesus Christ today,* and doing so in such a way that I never experience the reality of God without the reality of the world, nor the reality of the world without the reality of God.[3]

There is no division between the sacred and the secular. The reconciliation of Christ and the world at the cross is the foundation for Christian ethics. In the will and mission of God we find peace and reconciliation. Bonhoeffer's ethics of responsibility is central to his understanding of the church being Christ in the world. Through Christ's "vicarious representative action" (*Stellvertretung*) God acts in and through the incarnation, crucifixion and resurrection of Jesus Christ to reconcile humanity. For Bonhoeffer, the vicarious representative act of Christ on the cross has an incarnational dimension. God enters into our worldly context, in poverty and hiddenness, and is present in the reality of human suffering and pain. Therefore, the church is also called to act for the other and work toward reconciliation in and through the world.[4] This is not in an imitative manner based on Christ as model, but rather the church enters into God's presence and mission in the world.

Luther's description of freedom as always being "for the other" is a crucial criterion for Bonhoeffer's ethics. Freedom is always understood in a dialectical relationship with responsibility. In his most important work, *Ethics,* Bonhoeffer maintains that from the "outside" it is difficult to determine whether an action is responsible in a concrete case. The action may be "born from enthusiasm or legalism." However, he offers criteria for self-examination. The "field of responsibility" must be based not on principles but rather on "on the concrete call of Jesus alone." It should not be based on "character traits." If one is a "fanatic," there is danger in expanding one's call in the name of Jesus. Likewise, for one

---

[3]DBWE 6:55, emphasis added.
[4]DBWE 6:12.

who is cautious, insecure and legalistic, there is danger in "limiting responsibility to a narrow domain." The call to act responsibly is not centered in the self but rather in Christ's will.[5]

Bonhoeffer also cautions the church to refrain from an understanding of neighbors that is too narrowly defined. "Behind the neighbor, whom the call of Jesus commends to us, also stands, according to Jesus, the one who is farthest from us, namely, Jesus Christ himself who is indeed God."[6] He challenges the church to move beyond legalism to an embrace of those who do not share our same location, citizenship, profession or family. He gives as an example a legal case that occurred in 1931 in the United States. Nine black men were accused of raping a white girl. They were sentenced to death without any evidence that could prove their guilt. Bonhoeffer describes the outcome:

> This triggered a storm of outrage that found expression in open letters from the most respected European public figures. A Christian, disturbed by these events, asked a leading church official in Germany to consider raising his voice also in protest against this case. For his refusal to do so, the official cited the "Lutheran" understanding of vocation, that is, the limitation of the extent of his responsibility. But in fact it was protest from all around the world that eventually led to the revision of the verdict. Does the call of Jesus Christ itself lead us here to understand Nietzsche's statement: "My brothers, love of the neighbor I do not recommend to you: I recommend to you love of the farthest"?[7]

Bonhoeffer also describes the problem with churches and pastors refusing to assume the responsibility to speak out on behalf of the suffering and persecuted because they did not belong to their congregations. He argues that the definition of *neighbor* knows no boundaries. The church must always speak and act on behalf of others both close and far away. In loving the neighbor, the church loves Christ. Love of "the farthest" requires the church to act on behalf of the women and girls

---

[5]DBWE 6:294.
[6]Ibid.
[7]DBWE 6:295.

oppressed and abused, within both the local *and* the global community.

Freedom for the other, therefore, is always woven tightly to the meaning of responsibility and *Stellvertretung*. By way of immersion in Christ's mission, the church acts in responsibility for the other. The other is both the neighbor close in identity and the ones that are the farthest. In *Creation and Fall* Bonhoeffer describes freedom as never existing in a "vacuum." It is "not a quality of man, nor is it an ability, a capacity, a kind of being that somehow flares up in him. . . . It is not a possession, a presence, an object nor is it a form of existence—but a relationship and nothing else." He echoes Luther's understanding of freedom: freedom existing only in relationship. The dialectic of bondage and freedom in Christ informs the church how to be for the other.[8]

The theme of freedom is found throughout Bonhoeffer's work. Later, he relates the meaning of freedom to the political reality of Germany. In 1941, in response to the draft of a book,[9] Bonhoeffer describes the true meaning of freedom in a political context. This longer definition is worthy of the fuller quote:

> Being free *from* something is experienced only in being free *for* something. Being free solely in order to be free, however, leads to anarchy.
>
> Biblically, freedom means being free for service to God and to one's neighbor, being free for obedience to the commands of God. This presupposes being free from every internal and external pressure that hinders us in this service. Being free means, therefore, not the dissolution of all authority but living within the authorities and bonds ordered and *limited* by God's word.
>
> The question of individual freedoms—such as freedom of speech, freedom of the press, freedom of assembly, etc.—can be addressed only within this overarching context. The important question is the extent to which these freedoms are necessary and suited for fostering and securing freedom to live according to the commands of God. That is, freedom is in the first place not an *individual* right but a *responsibility;*

---

[8] Dietrich Bonhoeffer, *Creation and Fall* (New York: Touchstone Books, 1997), pp. 39-40.
[9] Bonhoeffer review of William Paton's *The Church and the New Order* (London: Student Christian Movement Press, 1941).

freedom is not in the first place oriented toward the individual but toward the neighbor.[10]

Bonhoeffer argues that the political results of his reflection on freedom are evident. The state has a responsibility to the commands of God and therefore must support the equal rights of all. Since the Nazi system, including and especially the Gestapo, are antithetical to God's will for freedom for all, they must be removed. The application of this ethical demand to always be free for the other has obvious political implications for the present-day situation in regard to the treatment of women and girls. Where states refuse to allow equal rights to women and girls, and also refuse them protection from violence, it is critical for the church to speak and act on behalf of the victims. The church must also oppose those systems, structures and states that act to oppose the freedoms granted by God.

CONFESSION AND RESISTANCE

Throughout church history there are events that bring about crisis for church identity and mission. The church of Germany during the Nazi regime found itself at a crossroads of church crisis that required great theological reflection on its very identity. It was necessary for the church to decide its path as a response to the deconfessionalism that Hitler demanded. There were those that argued for survival of the church by way of ignoring political realities and those, like Bonhoeffer, that fiercely defended the confession of the church by way of action and resistance. Before examining Bonhoeffer's response to systematic injustice, a general discussion of the role of confession is needed.

Roots of resistance to institutional systems that support evil begin in a foundational belief system. Christian identity is formed within the understanding and acceptance of the God we worship. Church identity is developed by confession of our God; subsequently, confession is an

---

[10]Dietrich Bonhoeffer, *Conspiracy and Imprisonment: 1940–1945*, trans. Lisa E. Dahill, ed. Larry L. Rasmussen, vol. 16 of *Dietrich Bonhoeffer Works—English Edition* (Minneapolis: Fortress Press, 2006), p. 532 (emphasis original).

expression of this identity.[11] Confession has a twofold nature: We confess our sinfulness, and in doing so we embrace the reality of God's grace. The declaration of one's condition and affirmation of God's mercy and love reveal the true nature of our relationship with God.

Therefore, confession of sin and confession in praise of God are only two sides of the same reality.[12] A statement of confession is necessary when the church is confronted by evil. Confessions act to stabilize and remind the church of the identity of this God whom we worship and obey. They have three primary functions. First, confessions proclaim God's grace. They are proclamations of God's love and Christ's saving work. Second, they identify the Christian community. Confessions remind believers of who they are in relation to God. In doing so, they create boundaries. When the church forgets its identity and fails in the task of setting limits, then it truly negates the necessity of the incarnation and cross of Christ. Alternatively, boundaries that are rigid become walls. These walls block the church from embracing its role in the world. The third function evolves from the second. Confessions remind the church of its prophetic role. This prophetic role cannot be established without boundaries. A church working within its present concrete worldly reality, sensitive to the mission of Christ, is in a position to voice its opposition to evil and work to establish justice. A church with rigid boundaries is in danger of turning inward on itself, turning from God's mission and rejecting its role in the world. Conversely, a church without boundaries is in danger of replacing the gospel with political ideologies (the ultimate and penultimate collapse) and confusing the roles of church and state.

Two confessional and theological motifs that support Christian action and resistance are expressed by the incarnation and a theology of the cross. Through the incarnation, God poured himself out for humankind through the birth, life and death of Jesus. His experiences and

---

[11]*Confession* is defined here as a communal statement of faith. The Augsburg Confession and Barmen Confession are examples.

[12]Bernhard Lohse, *A Short History of Christian Doctrine: From the First Century to the Present,* rev. ed., trans. F. Ernest Stoeffler (Philadelphia: Fortress, 1985), p. 165.

suffering were not merely "put on" but were fully human. God's revelation "was not a barrier to God's dealing with humanity, but precisely
the form which God chooses to act and speak in the world."[13] God
continues to work in and through history. The kingdom of God is both
beyond and within time and place. Christians are not called out of the
world but rather into the world for the sake of others. A theology of the
cross provides the lens through which to consider the role of suffering
in the Christian life. As described above, the theme of suffering is critical
in adopting a methodology for addressing the problem of violence
against women and girls. A theology of the cross undercuts Christian
theologies that accept the suffering endured by women victimized by
violence as redemptive. This is a type of "works righteousness" that fails
because it places the self in the role of Christ. It is Christ's suffering, and
no other, that broke the bondages of sin, death and hell. Only the suffering of Jesus has redemptive power and ultimately provides freedom
from pain and death. Suffering resulting from violence imposed on
women is not salvific but rather the consequence of sin.

The church has a responsibility to confess openly the freedom Christ
has gained for us through suffering already accomplished on the cross.
Those that impose suffering by oppression and violence through perverted teachings on submission, and by colluding with perpetrators, do
not understand the meaning of Christian suffering. Church leaders that
maintain the unity of families as a primary value, even when violence is
allowed to dominate women and girls, engage in idolatry of a patriarchal
system. Church silence and approval of violence against women, even
within the home, promote evil and are not in keeping with the Word of
God. Colluding with batterers and perpetrators of violence, and the institutions that support violence, in the name of love and loyalty is a false
loyalty. No person, ideology, institution, belief system or political
structure has a right or the power to subjugate and abuse in the name
of God "for the greater good."

---

[13]Clifford Green, "Introduction: Barth's Mature Theology," in *Karl Barth: Theologian of Freedom*, ed.
Clifford Green (Minneapolis: Fortress, 1991), p. 25.

Engagement in the liturgy is a continual reminder to the church of the God we worship and the church's identity as Christ in the world. This God we worship emptied himself of power for love of humanity. Colluding with those who claim power over others because of gender commits idolatry. The confessions of faith repeated during liturgy are powerful reminders that we are called to obey God alone. Loyalty to those that claim the power and authority to subjugate others is a false loyalty. Remembrance in the context of community provides a connection to the past. Becoming deeply connected to Christ and to each other takes great courage. Without the grace of Christ the truth would be devastating. It is truly a double-edged sword. Therefore, the process of remembering gives the Christian community direction and integrity.[14]

Community and confession were central themes for Dietrich Bonhoeffer.[15] Eberhard Bethge argued that confession clarified the church's identity but that it was not enough to combat evil. Confession must accompany resistance within the Christian community.

> Bonhoeffer introduced us in 1935 to the problem of what we today call political resistance. The levels of confession and of resistance could no longer be kept neatly apart. The escalating persecution of the Jews generated an increasingly intolerable situation, especially for Bonhoeffer himself. We now realized that mere confession, no matter how courageous, inescapably meant complicity with the murderers, even though there would always be new acts of refusing to be co-opted and even though we would preach "Christ alone" Sunday after Sunday. During the whole time the Nazi state never considered it necessary to prohibit such preaching. Why should it? Thus we were approaching the borderline between confession and resistance; and if we did not cross this border, our confession was going to be no better than cooperation with the

---

[14]Bethge, *Friendship and Resistance*, p. 105.

[15]Bonhoeffer closely aligns the church community with the incarnate Christ. "The Body of Jesus Christ is identical with the new humanity which he has assumed. The body of Christ is his church-community [*Gemeinde*]. Jesus Christ at the same time is himself and his church community (I Cor. 12.12)." Dietrich Bonhoeffer, *Discipleship*, trans. Reinhard Krauss and Barbara Green, ed. John D. Godsey and Geffrey B. Kelly, vol. 4 of *Dietrich Bonhoeffer Works—English Edition* (Minneapolis: Fortress, 2003), pp. 217-18.

criminals. And so it became clear where the problem lay for the Confessing Church: We were resisting by way of confession, but we were not confessing by way of resistance.[16]

Bonhoeffer believed that the confession of the suffering Christ is the foundation for action. He was a theologian and an activist. Indeed, his theology necessitated his resistance. Confession without resistance becomes an instrument of collusion with evil when we denounce evil acts but refuse to work toward ending them. Bonhoeffer did not lose his identity in Christ by his engagement in the world, nor did he refuse this involvement because of this identity.

> People today who confine themselves to confession and never cross the threshold often ask how a man like Bonhoeffer could theologically justify his identification with the conspirators. The question is frightful, because it is usually raised out of an isolated and isolating situation of detached confessionalism, unconscious of its own complicity with evil. My wife once gave the shortest answer: How can a confessing Christian theologically justify a lack of action?[17]

How does the church discern the nature of resistance to the present realities of evil? It is community that provides the context in which confession and resistance receive nurture and direction. The church community provides the context for consciousness raising, theological reflection and exploration of avenues of resistance toward evil. The role of confessions as dynamic statements of belief is central in the theology and ethic of Dietrich Bonhoeffer. There were many contributing factors that led to Bonhoeffer's decision to engage in acts of resistance. Nevertheless, Bonhoeffer reminds us of the role of confession in the task of ending violence against women. Proclamation of the gospel as the basis for social justice practice is clearly exemplified by Bonhoeffer's ethic and his resistance activity.

The role of confession within the church struggle with National So-

---

[16]Bethge, *Friendship and Resistance*, p. 24.
[17]Ibid., p. 27.

cialism is profoundly significant. It reveals a means by which the Confessing Church proclaimed Christ as the only source of God's revelation, created boundaries between the true church and state with its false religion, and provided the basis for a prophetic voice of resistance.

> In the light of the history of dogma, what is the significance of this struggle? It is to be found in the fact that the church gave an account of itself regarding the sources of its proclamation and its doctrine, that it publicly confessed these foundations of its faith in a new way, and that it thereby drew lines of demarcation not only between itself and the totalitarian state of the Third Reich with its neo-paganism, but also between itself and all attempts to regard certain historical events, or a certain natural, racial disposition of man, as the norm or content of preaching. The Confessing Church's opposition to National Socialism and its insistence upon law and justice were important, to be sure. Yet from the point of view of the history of dogma the real fruit of the church's recent struggle is to be found in its new and unprecedented reflection on God's revelation in Jesus Christ as distinct from all other kinds of revelation.[18]

Dietrich Bonhoeffer lived out his theology in his struggle and resistance to the evil that was infecting his church and his world. He was rooted in a confessional theology that steadied and centered him in Christ. His understanding of God's faithfulness and the identity of the Christian church did not allow him to be seduced into colluding with evil or withdrawing from the struggle into safety. Bonhoeffer's use of the language of the cross is instrumental in constructing a methodology for addressing institutional and social violence against women and girls in any form. Repentance, forgiveness and reconciliation are key themes that have meaning within the context of the proclamation of Christ as Savior. Bethge utilizes the language of the cross in the primary concepts of confession and resistance. The language provides a theological perspective of the cross and a conceptual framework that connect theology and ethics. The church in Nazi Germany faced a di-

---

[18]Lohse, *Short History of Christian Doctrine*, p. 232.

lemma when confronted with evil. Dietrich Bonhoeffer and many others were able to remember and clearly articulate their beliefs through confession. Rooted in confession and conversion, they resisted evil and promoted the gospel of love. There were those who forgot and denied their true identity as a people of God. They colluded with corrupt power. Some chose violence. Others withdrew and became silent. Bonhoeffer resisted the seduction of self-preservation and chose to confess Christ within a worldly reality of the true gospel. Consequently, he became the enemy of those who wielded crushing political power.

> Confession cannot worry about success or failure. It lives only by him whom it confesses, the crucified and risen one. Confession is a public matter. It spells out openly the name of Christ and publicly refuses praise for any other kind of messiah, whether of Teutonic, Eastern or Western origin. It is wary of any co-optation of the church; for the desire of society and the powers to co-opt the churches for their own purposes is never absent, however subtly or not so subtly this may manifest itself. Confession seeks the pulpit and if necessary the courtroom, not in order to make a show, but to give a clear and unambiguous message.[19]

On the day of the election of pro-Nazi leaders for the new German Protestant Church in July 1933, Bonhoeffer preached a sermon that outlined the church's struggle to find its identity and confess its faith. He developed his sermon from Matthew 16:13-18, in which Jesus confronts Peter with the question, "Who do you say that I am?"

> The Church of Peter—that means the church of rock, the church of confessing Christ. The church of Peter is not the church of opinions and views but rather the church of revelation; not the church that talks about "what people say" but the church in which Peter's confession is always being made and spoken anew, the church that does nothing else but always and only makes this confession, whether in singing, praying, preaching, or action. It is the church that only stands on the rock as long as it keeps doing this, but becomes the house built on sand that the wind

---

[19]Bethge, *Friendship and Resistance*, pp. 26-27.

blows down if it dares to think of going another way, for whatever reason, or even to look away for a moment.[20]

Bonhoeffer notes that Peter and the church fail because of weakness, fear and seduction by the world. Therefore, confession of the true Christ is critical for the church to stay a church.

> Yet it is not we who are to build, but God. No human being builds the church, but Christ alone. Anyone who proposes to build the church is certainly already on the way to destroying it, because it will turn out to be a temple of idolatry, though the builder does not intend that or know it. We are to confess, while God builds. We are to preach, while God builds. We are to pray to God, while God builds. We do not know God's plan. We cannot see whether God is building up or taking down. It could be that the times that human beings judge to be times for knocking down structures would be, for God, times to do a lot of building, or that the great moments of the church from a human viewpoint are, for God, times for pulling it down. It is a great comfort that Christ gives to the church: "You confess, preach, bear witness to me, but I alone will do the building, wherever I am pleased to do so. Don't interfere with my orders. Church, if you do your own part right, then that is enough. But make sure you do it right. Don't look for anyone's opinion; don't ask them what they think. Don't keep calculating; don't look around for support from others. Not only must church remain church, but you, my church, confess, confess, confess." . . . Christ alone is your Lord; by his grace alone you live, just as you are. Christ is building.[21]

This is a clear challenge for the church today! The work to end violence against women and girls is a challenge to the Christian churches— impacting its reputation, distribution of resources, political affiliations and willingness to embrace a radical discipleship and to disavow a comfortable identification with wealth and political power. Identifying with victims of violence is where Christ resides and where the church must

---

[20]Dietrich Bonhoeffer, *Berlin: 1932–1933*, trans. Isabel Best and David Higgins, ed. Larry L. Rasmussen, vol. 12 of *Dietrich Bonhoeffer Works—English Edition* (Minneapolis: Fortress, 2009), p. 479.
[21]DBWE 12:480-81.

exist. Bonhoeffer's prophetic call for the church to "confess, confess, confess," no matter the consequences, has profound ramifications for a church called to speak against the objectification of women and girls, patriarchy, and gendercide.

Bonhoeffer finishes his sermon by reminding the church that, although all may appear lost, victory is in reality at hand because Christ has given victory by overcoming death. The message is for the church to have faith and hope in the ongoing work of Christ. He sums up: "'Fear not, little flock, for it is your Father's good pleasure to give you the kingdom.' 'For where two or three are gathered in my name, there am I in the midst of them.' The city of God stands on a firm foundation."[22]

Therefore, confessions identify the church and are in themselves acts of resistance. By proclaiming Christ and staying true to God's call to be disciples, the Christian church separates itself from evil and serves God alone. This is a form of resistance. The Confessing Church's motive for its early confessions was not to resist the Nazi state but rather to assert its identity in Jesus Christ. They were concerned with confessing the faith in the new challenging situation. Resistance was not in their vocabulary in the early years.

> Faith and not politics, confession and not resistance, was at the root of our understanding of *status confessionis*, which gave us the courage to take risks. Getting diverted into political issues could only weaken our confession of the one Christ—of that we were certain for quite some time. As young Lutherans in 1934 we were totally unprepared for something like political resistance. We had neither experience with nor conceptions of such activities. And frankly, most of us still believed during Hitler's first years that his efforts and goals were in the best interests of Germany. When this belief began to be shaken, nobody spoke of resistance, even less so when some conscious acts of resistance were in fact committed.[23]

---

[22]DBWE 12:481.
[23]Bethge, *Friendship and Resistance*, pp. 19-20.

Bonhoeffer was one of the first to identify the need to move beyond confession toward resistance. While acknowledging the power of confession as statements of protest, he was aware of the danger of a confessionalism that did not also voice opposition to evil. In August 1933, the Bethel Confession was written by a small group of pastors within the *Reichskirche*.[24] Its purpose was to offer support to groups working in opposition to the Nazi government. However, Bonhoeffer refused to sign because he believed that it did not go far enough in support of the Jews.[25] During the same period he was discouraged and disappointed over the failure of pastors to resign from the state church over the implementation of the Aryan Clause.[26] However, the Bethel Confession has significance for the church today. The August 1933 version of the Bethel Confession[27] addresses the marks and boundaries of the Christian church. In distinguishing the limitations of the government to determine church identity and membership, it rejects the racist attempt to convert the German Protestant church into a Reich church for Aryans.

> The fellowship of those belonging to the church is determined not by blood nor, therefore, by race, but by the Holy Spirit and baptism.... We object to the attempt to make the German Protestant church into a Reich church for Christians of the Aryan race, thus robbing it of its promise.... The Christians who are of Gentile descent must be prepared to expose themselves to persecution before they are ready to betray in even a single case, voluntarily or under compulsion, the church's fellowship with Jewish Christians that is instituted in Word and sacrament.[28]

The message of the gospel is given for all people no matter gender, race or nationality. The proclamation of Christ crosses all boundaries and must not be exclusive in its membership or outreach.

---

[24]DBWE 12:374-424.

[25]Bethge, *Friendship and Resistance*, p. 59, n. 71.

[26]John W. de Gruchy, "The Development of Bonhoeffer's Theology," in Dietrich Bonhoeffer, *Dietrich Bonhoeffer: Witness to Jesus Christ*, ed. John W. de Gruchy (Minneapolis: Fortress, 1987), p. 21.

[27]Bonhoeffer drafted the August version of the Bethel Confessions in Berlin. He later rejected the November revisions. See DBWE 12:374, editor's note 1.

[28]DBWE 12:419-21.

The message of the gospel is equally accessible, or equally inaccessible, to all peoples. For it is only God's Holy Spirit who can bring about faith in human beings and awaken consensus on the true confession. The communion of the confessing church extends across the borders between peoples. The boundaries of the Volk and church are never the same.[29]

Gender should not be a determining factor for membership in the church, or for deciding roles within the church. Determination of both is given by the gift of faith and the calling of the Holy Spirit. Too often the exclusion of women from ministerial roles is argued from a position of "orders of creation." Violence against women and girls has often been justified within the church with the same argument for excluding Jewish Christians from the church during the time of the Reich church. Never can race, gender, ethnicity or national origin be the determinant for full membership and access to all ministry positions. It is Christ alone who calls and is the giver of all abilities and vocation.

On May 29 to 31, 1934, the Confessing Church held its first synod at Barmen. The message of the Barmen Declaration, as a response to the growing deconfessionalization of the church under Hitler, was to proclaim that the demands of the gospel of Jesus Christ cannot accommodate cultural norms and political ideologies that violate the supremacy of God's rule of love.

The focus of Barmen was both proclamation and opposition. This confession proclaimed Christ as the source of God's truth and revelation and rejected any other power, truths or historical figures as that source.

Here, as in the condemnations which are added to other statements, it becomes clear that the church has its foundation in Jesus Christ alone, and that it is under no obligation to proclaim anything other than the gospel of Jesus Christ, that, indeed, it recognizes no other sources for its faith but the Word of God.[30]

---

[29]DBWE 12:412.
[30]Lohse, *Short History of Christian Doctrine*, p. 234.

Every declaration regarding the true identity of the church and its role is followed by a rejection of false doctrine promulgated by the German Christians and the Nazi state. Barmen clearly states the confession of the Christian church and its opposition to false doctrines. The Barmen Declaration was decidedly an act of resistance. There are always consequences to acts of resistance. Barth was suspended from teaching in November of 1934 and then forbidden to speak in public. He soon returned to Switzerland. Punishment by the state came swiftly for many. "That Declaration was the character of the resistance. Rather than deny it, men lost their livelihood, accepted harsh imprisonment, were exiled and some resisted unto death."[31] The whole of the Confessing Church grew uneasy as a result of stepping into unknown and treacherous territory.

> Suddenly there were hints that our acts of confession might touch on other dimensions. At first we noted only vague hints, which we thought it best to put out of our mind. But a certain uneasiness persisted: that with the step into the *status confessionis* the "whole question of justice and righteousness in the Third Reich" could at one point be directed against us, the confessing Christians, the church, the public.[32]

The Second Synod at Dahlem rejected the official church government and took a stand on church order.[33] Both Barmen and Dahlem were significant because they fulfilled the second function of a confessing church. They set boundaries. By proclaiming the Confessing Church's identity in Christ and rejecting false doctrines it upheld the faith. This was not so much an attempt to keep people out as to mark the perimeters of the true church in this new situation. It was the burden of the German Christians to choose to reenter the true church or remain outside.

> Then question then is: What did God say about his church when he spoke through Barmen and Dahlem? The government of the National Church

---

[31]Edwin Robertson, *The Shame and the Sacrifice: The Life and Martyrdom of Dietrich Bonhoeffer* (New York: Collier Books, 1988), p. 117.

[32]Bethge, *Friendship and Resistance*, pp. 20-21.

[33]Gruchy, "Development of Bonhoeffer's Theology," p. 22.

has cut itself off from the Christian church. The Confessing Church is the true church of Jesus Christ in Germany. What does that mean? It undoubtedly means that a definitive boundary has been recognized and confirmed between the government of the National Church and the true church of Christ. The government of the National Church is heretical.[34]

CHURCH AND STATE BOUNDARIES

It is vital for the church to move beyond confession to acts of resistance, or the church's confession of faith is impotent. Embracing the truths of the gospel of Jesus Christ creates a prophetic voice that rejects evil and provides possibilities for community reflection and action. Within this context, deeper analysis of the boundaries between church and state is possible. This analysis is critical for the church to consider a response to violations of these boundaries. This is the path that Bonhoeffer followed, that is, a move from confession to resistance against a state that violated its boundaries and counted heinous acts against its citizens. Dietrich Bonhoeffer's concept of the relationship of church and state has important applications in considering a contemporary church response to violence against women and girls. Bonhoeffer argued that both church and state are part of the kingdom of God. Each has its role, but both are to live out their roles responsibly. In his essay "The Church and the Jewish Question,"[35] Bonhoeffer warns of the dangers of the state either exerting too much law and interfering with church matters, or too little law, resulting in a lack of human rights protections. Too much law means that the state uses "too much force" and inhibits the church from proclaiming its gospel message. Too little law results in a group being deprived of its rights.[36] Either too little law and order or too much law and order compels the church to speak.[37] Bonhoeffer's descriptions of church-and-state boundaries have direct applications to

---

[34]Dietrich Bonhoeffer, "The Question of the Boundaries of the Church and Church Union," in Bonhoeffer, *Dietrich Bonhoeffer: Witness to Jesus Christ*, p. 151.

[35]DBWE 12:361-70.

[36]DBWE 12:364-65.

[37]DBWE 12:364.

the role of the state in either colluding with perpetrators of violence by not protecting the rights of women and girls (too little law) or being an instrument of violence (too much law).

There are nuances in Bonhoeffer's argument that are worth exploring, especially when applying his theological ethics to a possible contemporary church response to the problem of violence against women and children. He distinguishes individuals and "humanitarian associations" from "the true church of Christ" when considering a legitimate response to a state that either exerts too much law or not enough law, whereby causing suffering and oppression. Bonhoeffer maintained that individuals and associations are needed to "moralize" and provide accusations against the state whenever it fails in its role to protect and act as a moral agent. However, he claims that this is not the role of the "true church of Christ." The church cannot take direct political action against the state. However, the church must not be silent. The church must strongly question the state as to whether "its actions can be justified as legitimate state actions."[38] However, the church can ultimately engage in direct political action *if* the state refuses its role, and the church must, paradoxically, save the state from itself.

Therefore, in this way Bonhoeffer challenges Hitler's anti-Semitic laws and lays the foundation for direct church action against the state. He proposes three ways in which the church can respond to the state. First, it can challenge the authorities and their actions, and put the responsibility back on the state to act in a "legitimate" fashion. Second, the church can aid victims of the persecution. "The church has an unconditional obligation toward the victims of any societal order even if they do not belong to the Christian community. Let us work for the good of all."[39] The Christian church is committed to love its neighbors both within and outside of the church. Bonhoeffer argues that the church may never abandon these two duties. The third response has to do with direct acts of resistance.

---

[38]DBWE 12:363-64.
[39]DBWE 12:365.

The *third* possibility is not just to bind up the wounds of the victims beneath the wheel but to seize the wheel itself. Such an action would be direct political action on the part of the church. This is only possible and called for if the church sees the state to be failing in its function of creating law and order, that is, if the church perceives that the state, without any scruples, has created either too much or too little law and order. It must see in either eventuality a threat to the existence of the state and thus to its own existence as well. There would be too little if any one group of citizens is deprived of its rights. There would be too much in the case of an attack, coming from the state, on the nature of the church and its proclamation, such as the obligatory exclusion of baptized Jews from our Christian congregations or a ban on missions to the Jews. In such a case, the church would find itself in *statu confessionis,* and the state would find itself in the act of self-negation. A state that incorporates a church that it has violated has lost its most loyal servant.[40]

Bonhoeffer is well aware of the serious nature of this third response. He advises that a decision for direct political acts of resistance "be decided by an 'evangelical council' as and when the occasion arises and hence cannot be casuistically construed beforehand."[41] Acts of resistance are always decided within the context of community. Bonhoeffer's acts of resistance are statements of confession. Therefore, they are acts that proclaim Jesus as the only Lord of the church, and they uphold the dignity and integrity of the community of humanity. They are salt and light that point to a God who is full of compassion and love. Confession *and* resistance against evil are both necessary for the church of Christ to remain the church.

These confessions are powerful words of remembrance. Nazi Germany was a place that the church was challenged by strong opponents and forces to accept false doctrine. Confessions, lectures, letters and sermons by Bonhoeffer and others were all attempts to remind the Christian community of the character of God and the church. They knew that the failure to stand firmly on Christ, the Rock, would mean

---

[40]DBWE 12:365-66.
[41]DBWE 12:367.

the erosion of the church's identity and mission. The temptation and danger of colluding with evil was overwhelming. During a time of confusion the confessions acted to remind and direct the church.

Bonhoeffer recognized the possibility that idolatry was not limited to the adulation of evil but, more dangerously, might lead to the displacement of Christ in order to engage in the worshiping of "the good." Within his context, the colluding church was venerated even though it was rejecting the gospel.

> To reject the political system of that time in theory, to reject it by withdrawing into a spiritual realm, was not enough for him. Such an attitude was schizophrenia, it meant that the challenge was not taken seriously; it meant just talk not action. That in the first instance the Church fought for its own preservation filled him with sorrow. In a situation where millions of people were threatened in their very existence, it was not a question of saving the Church. But it was mankind that had to be saved. The very conviction that made him a man of peace, led him into the resistance.[42]

Bethge argues that confession and resistance against evil are two necessary but separate functions of a faithful community.[43] Confession alone can be a form of resistance. However, confession without acts of resistance can be perverted into a supportive force for evil. "By leaving out the steps from confession to resistance, one ends up tolerating crimes, turning confession into an alibi and, in view of the injustice committed, an indictment of the confessors."[44] This is an example of Luther's condemnation of faith without works. Confession, which occurs within the context of community, is co-opted when community refuses to act in opposition to evil. Collusion is particularly insidious because it often presents itself as a self-righteous and pious Christianity. This is seductive to a church community. It offers the comfortable illusion for members that they are a faithful church.

---

[42]Robertson, *Shame and the Sacrifice,* pp. 195-96.
[43]Bethge, *Friendship and Resistance,* p. 32.
[44]Ibid., p. 28.

In fact, a church that confesses to follow Christ alone and yet allows for the destruction of others is as responsible for the effects of evil acts as the instigators. A colluding church also participates in its own destruction. The model depicts the eventual consequences for colluding with the enemy. On a personal level, one may become more grounded in denial and subsequently more involved in treacherous acts. On an institutional level, collusion leads to violence and separation from (forgetting) the gospel.

An important step between confession and resistance (faith and action) is identification with the persecuted. This understanding rooted in Christ's "representative vicarious action" challenges the church to be Christ in the world. In "carrying the cross" the church commits to both confession and action on behalf of the powerless, oppressed and suffering. "The point in which confession which refuses co-optation is joined by the perception of the persecuted represents the threshold of political resistance."[45] Once the confessing Christian passes this threshold, the confession does not simply disappear, although for quite a while it may hardly be heard. It remains alive, however hidden, with him whom it confesses. And this is of special importance in the moment of the failure of resistance, of defeat and discouragement or of the necessary healing of that which resistance had to destroy or wound.[46]

A confessional church that identifies and embraces the persecuted is unable to turn away and withdraw into silence and collusion. Bonhoeffer's movement toward resistance paralleled his increasing solidarity with the Jews. Hitler divided church leadership by allowing pastors to remain "neutral." They could preach the gospel and uphold the church confessions as long as they did not interfere with state politics. Many pastors adopted this stance and thereby colluded with the oppressors. Bonhoeffer became more committed to moving away from a confessionalism that was unwilling to engage in political acts of resistance.[47]

---

[45]Ibid., p. 27.
[46]Ibid.
[47]Gruchy, "Development of Bonhoeffer's Theology," p. 22.

Karl Barth, writing in 1967, when he had read Eberhard Bethge's classic biography of Dietrich Bonhoeffer, recalled with shame that Bonhoeffer had spoken out more clearly and much earlier than any of them about the treatment of the Jews—as fellow human beings, not simply when they were also fellow Christians. At that time, Barth reminds his readers, the Evangelical Churches were more concerned with self-preservation than the awful injustice done to the Jews. It was this that started Bonhoeffer's disillusion with even the Confessing Church and turned him towards a political action which was alien to him.[48]

Bonhoeffer could not envision a church that would oppose evil only in theory and not in practice. Discipleship required a practical application of the gospel. Living out the faith meant acting for the other, for the persecuted, and opposing in deed those who promulgated evil. In *The Cost of Discipleship,* Bonhoeffer writes of the necessity of the church to fulfill its call as a light to others.[49] This cannot be only preached from the pulpit; rather, it must be acted out in the world.

Again, it is not enough to teach the law of Christ, it must be done, otherwise it is no better than the old law. In what follows, the disciples are told how to practice this righteousness of Christ. It extends beyond following Christ as model. It means being Christ in the world. It is the real and active faith in the righteousness of Christ. It is the new law, the law of Christ.[50]

BONHOEFFER'S THEOLOGY OF SUFFERING

Like Luther, Dietrich Bonhoeffer's theology of the cross does not focus on the philosophical approach to theodicy. Although theodicy was most certainly a concern, his focus was on more pragmatic issues related to the problem of suffering.[51] Bonhoeffer's approach to the effects of suffering on the person and community is a result of his engagement

---

[48]Robertson, *Shame and the Sacrifice,* p. 37.
[49]DBWE 4:112-14.
[50]DBWE 4:120.
[51]See Annette G. Aubert's essay, "Theodicy and the Cross and the Theology of Dietrich Bonhoeffer," *Trinity Journal* 32 NS (2011): 47. See n. 1 for a short bibliography of recent research on Bonhoeffer and theodicy.

with those who were personally impacted by racism, violence and oppression. He centered the problem of evil within his Christology and
perspective of the cross.[52]

Luther's theology of the cross informed and shaped Bonhoeffer's understanding of the significance of the cross and suffering. The transcendent God is known only through the "hidden revelation." God's
self-revelation was through the historical event of the incarnation, crucifixion and resurrection of Jesus Christ. God can only be known
through suffering and the cross. God entered into the suffering of
humankind, and it is there that we encounter this God, who is truly love
in reality. Paradoxically, this transcendent, all-powerful God is the weak
God known to us only by way of our turning from self toward the suffering and rejected Other. Both Luther and Barth emphasize the transcendent God. Likewise, for Bonhoeffer, God is truly transcendent.
Nevertheless, Bonhoeffer claimed that God is "grasped only in his
worldly interactions."[53] Bonhoeffer's year in New York (1930–1931) was
significant in shaping his response to racism and the systemic supports
for social injustice. It was during his time in Harlem attending church
services and in his discussions with African American leaders struggling
with justice issues in a uniquely American context that he was able to
reflect deeply on the costs of human idolatry and sin. Christ was present
with those who endured the hardships brought on by racism whether
the oppressed were African Americans in the United States or the Jews
in Europe. The transcendent God was also the hidden Christ found
serving those who were marginalized and rejected.

In his July 16, 1944, letter to Eberhard Bethge, Bonhoeffer summarized the way that God has chosen to be in the world. Subsequently, it
is the only way God *is now* present with us.

> God lets himself be pushed out of the world on to the cross. He is weak
> and powerless in the world, and this is precisely the way, the only way in
> which he is with us and helps us. Matt. 8.17 makes it quite clear that

---

[52]Ibid., p. 48.
[53]Ibid., p. 52.

> Christ helps us, not by virtue of his omnipotence, but by virtue of his
> weakness and suffering.[54]

In humility, the church is present and "for the other." The crusading
Christ with a crusading church is replaced by the Christ of the cross and
a repentant and suffering-servant church.

Therefore, human beings can only regain their freedom through Jesus'
work on the cross. Or in Luther's language, through bondage to Christ,
we are truly free. Where then do we find this Christ? Bonhoeffer, as
Luther before him, maintained that Christ is found in the hidden, unexpected place: the Word, sacrament and true church. Christ is not
found in the triumphal church that identifies with nationalism but
rather with the weak, humble community of the suffering. Christ is
found in the world reality of the ordinary and concrete. Christ is received only through the unexpected and surprising gift of faith.
Therefore, like Luther, Bonhoeffer rejects the philosophical and rational
solutions to the problem of evil.[55] Also, in accordance with Luther,
attempting to determine the reasons for evil is not the task for the
theologian of the cross. God's righteousness was manifest on the cross.
Humankind is responsible for the evil it inflicts on itself. Through the
cross and resurrection, suffering, evil and death will ultimately be
overcome. As Christ identifies with humanity through the suffering on
the cross, so he continues to identify at the present time with those who
suffer. Bonhoeffer does not need to justify God regarding the problem
of evil. It is humankind that needs to be justified. Through the cross and
resurrection God overcomes the enemy and triumphs over evil. That
reality may be hidden in the present suffering of the world, but it is
indeed completely true. Hope and joy are able to exist within the
context of suffering because the hidden God continues to be present
and, ultimately, triumphs over evil.

Bonhoeffer understands Christ as present in the suffering, but on a

---

[54]Dietrich Bonhoeffer, *Letters and Papers from Prison*, ed. Eberhard Bethge (New York: Collier Books,
1971), pp. 360-61.
[55]Aubert, "Theodicy and the Cross," p. 55.

deeper level he identifies Christ as the suffering God who calls all to enter into his sufferings. Bonhoeffer's answer to the problem of theodicy is the *theologia crucis*.[56] In the horrific suffering of the Holocaust the crucified Christ is truly found within that reality. Bonhoeffer rejects an abstract theory to the solution of theodicy. He directs the church to the cross and offers a practical and strategic response: enter into the suffering of others and there will be found the suffering Christ, hidden to those without faith. There, on the cross, is also found hope. The faithful church is a church of the cross living the hope and reality of the resurrection. A nationalistic and triumphal church knows nothing of the suffering Christ because it rejects the call of Christ to love others by way of being present with their suffering.

Jesus' call to "take up your cross" is the only way into discipleship (see Lk 9:23). Christ's entrance into the world dispels the notion of two realities: the church and the world. There is one reality in Christ and in Christ "all things exist" (Heb 2:10). For Bonhoeffer, true discipleship requires that we bring the good news of hope and redemption to the world. It also requires that we be responsible for our neighbor, and for each person we encounter and for those far away. We encounter the suffering Christ in the other's suffering, and we are called to enter into that suffering and be Christ to the world.

Bonhoeffer is realistic in his ethic. He does not believe that the church can solve every social problem. Nevertheless, he calls the church to enter into the work and suffering of Christ in the world. The work of Christ in the world and subsequently the work in the church are identical. There is no room for a detached theology and ethic; neither is it possible to create a type of "Christian kingdom" in the world. Bonhoeffer only calls the church to be faithful to the God it claims and responsible and obedient to Christ's mission and call in the world.

Christ enters into suffering and is known through suffering as he is known through all of human life. Christ's identification with the outcast, the poor, the misunderstood, the suffering and the oppressed answers

---

[56]Ibid., p. 62.

the question, "Where is God?" God is found among "the least of these" (Mt 25). Luther's God *pro me, pro nobis* is for Bonhoeffer always for the other. The work of Christ is in feeding the hungry, freeing the oppressed and binding up the wounds of the brokenhearted. Exactly as Christ was found in the concrete reality of the suffering of those victimized in the concentration camps, Christ is also found in the gendercide of the twenty-first century. The suffering, living Christ is present among the suffering of the millions of women and girls who are oppressed because of their gender. God is found among those women and girls who continue to suffer because God is always found among "the least of these."

A CHALLENGE TO THE CHURCH

The central roles of confession and resistance in Bonhoeffer's theology and ethic are extremely vital issues for the contemporary church. The question Jesus posed to Peter, "Who do you say that I am?" (Mt 16:15), was the critical question that Bonhoeffer put before the church in Nazi Germany. As discussed above, Bonhoeffer viewed the role of the church as confessing and proclaiming Christ as Lord. Confessions acted to remind the church then, as they do today, who Christ is and who we are in relation to God. There is always the danger of the church being side-tracked and seduced by other philosophies, gods, and cultural and political ideologies. Confessions continue to remind the church of its identity and purpose in Christ. They also create boundaries that should always be open for "the farthest." But they also act to clearly mark the differences between a false church and the true church. Bonhoeffer was not timid concerning this point. He did not hesitate to condemn as heretical those who supported Nazi policies.[57] This position is relevant and applicable to our current situation of gendercide. Those who opposed apartheid in South Africa are indebted to Bonhoeffer's application of Luther's theology of the cross for helping to formulate a church response. When a church adopts views in opposition to the gospel, then it also draws the line between the false and true church. "A more con-

---

[57]Bonhoeffer, "Boundaries of Church and Church Union," p. 151.

temporary example of this recognition of boundaries, in many respects influenced by Bonhoeffer's insights, has been the declaration that 'apartheid is a heresy.' The boundaries of the 'true church' have been determined in response to the racism of the 'false church' or the world."[58]

Bonhoeffer maintains that confessionalism reminds the church of sin (both personal and communal). The community acknowledges, in prayerful confession, that there is but one Lord. This acts as a reminder of the many times in which we have served other gods. These gods may take many forms: other persons, money, addictions, self, good causes, political parties or materialism. As we confess, individually and as a community, we are brought to a place of repentance and conversion (in the language of the cross). Without confession and conversion, we as humans will inevitably deny our sin and collude with evil. Confession glorifies God and humbles members of the faithful community. The willingness to remember sin and recognize the need for forgiveness is essential before judging others' sins. The church must continually confess, recognize its sin and turn once again to Christ. Confession is pivotal in this process. From this place, the church can use its prophetic voice with power and authority. It realizes that its power and authority do not come from a sinless state but rather from a gracious and merciful God.

Bonhoeffer's exhortation to his fellow brothers and sisters and his condemnation of the National Church did not originate from a self-righteous and self-promoting disposition. He recognized his own faults and the shortcomings of the Confessing Church. His willingness to judge and condemn heresy was deeply rooted in faith in a Christ who holds all power and authority. This is significant today. There may be a tendency in the church today to shy away from the language of the cross, including *sin, heresy, false church, remembrance, confession* and *conversion*. Political ideologies replace theology as the starting point for action, and they seduce the church into complacency and relinquishing its prophetic role. Many Christians forgot their identity in Christ, opened their door to Nazi ideology and colluded with a destructive evil. A con-

---

[58]Gruchy, "Development of Bonhoeffer's Theology," p. 24.

fessional community is able to condemn sin not because it is without fault but rather because Christ, who is without blemish, reveals and condemns that which is evil and false. Bonhoeffer's message serves as a warning to the church. A faithful church cannot serve two masters. The sovereignty of God always supersedes the world.

> Bonhoeffer's protest, which set off a chain of events that finally brought him to the gallows, was essentially a protest about the deformation of the church. The Nazis, as we all know, wanted to remake the church according to their own ideological predilections. Barth, Bonhoeffer, and others of the Confessing Church recognized early on that the struggle with the Nazis was a struggle for the integrity and faithfulness of the church. To say "no" when and how they did was a public, political act. It demonstrated that there is a reality (God) that transcends the state and a message (the Gospel) that is inviolable. Such a witness carried dire consequences. So, instead of "the world setting the agenda for the church," as the disastrous slogan of the sixties had it, God sets the agenda for the church by giving it a clear and pointed calling.[59]

However, confessionalism alone is not enough to combat evil. Bonhoeffer warned of the danger of confessionalism without resistance. This is Luther's same warning against faith without works. This too is significant when considering the mandate to action the church should take in addressing the problem of violence against women. Confessing without action can lead to a paralyzing institutionalization of the gospel. Bonhoeffer's confessionalism was alive because he applied it to the crises of his situation.

We are not battling National Socialism. How can the church apply the lessons learned from Bonhoeffer? Specifically, are there lessons to be learned from the work and theology of the cross of Bonhoeffer and the Confessing Church that can be applied to the issue of violence against women and girls in much the same way as many churches did in addressing racism and apartheid? Bonhoeffer's recommended re-

---

[59]Robert Benne, "The Lutheran Tradition and Public Theology," *Lutheran Theological Seminary Bulletin* 76 (1995): 19.

sponses of the church to a state that takes too much power or allows lawlessness are helpful in evaluating this contemporary situation. When the state power impedes the work of the church, or is self-destructive, the church has a responsibility to act. Bonhoeffer suggests the first response should be direct response to the government (a call for justice), and the second, to aid the victims of state action. These two can be easily applied to current situations of violence against women in parts of the world where laws protecting women are inconsistently and infrequently enforced, or do not exist at all. The church must continue to cry out against injustice and aid those persecuted and oppressed. The third response involves direct political action against an evil system or state government. This may be straightforward in a situation that calls the church to define a situation as *status confessionis,* such as the policy of apartheid in South Africa (condemned as heretical).

At first glance the serious injustice of gendercide would not appear to fit into a situation of crisis and heresy. Overt support of gender violence by church denominations is sporadic. Nevertheless, I would argue that widespread covert support exists in areas where female genital mutilation, forced abortions and sterilizations, female infanticide, domestic violence, female slavery, forced prostitution, and mass rapes and sexual assaults as tools of war remain a part of the political and cultural fabric of life for women. There is little or no condemnation and resistance work offered by churches in many parts of the world. The gospel is distorted and undermined when there is systemic violence perpetrated against women as a consequence of their gender. What should the church's response be to the widespread problem of violence against women and girls? Many are responding. But so much more can be done. Bonhoeffer's theology and activism expose the evil of racism, collusion and denial that continue to seduce a complacent church. His message is as relevant today as it was in the last century. The church need not abandon the language and theology of the cross in order to condemn violence against women and work to establish justice. It is because of the cross of Christ that the churches must resolve to condemn the destruction of women's lives and consider violence against women a matter of grave sin and heresy. Luther's theology of the cross and Bonhoeffer's contemporary example of applying that theology provide the critical framework for a methodology that challenges the church to live out its mandate to proclaim the gospel by both confession and resistance.

6

CREATIVE THEOLOGICAL REFLECTION AND ACTIVISM

Working to End Gendercide

IMAGINE. IMAGINE A THEOLOGICAL APPROACH to ending violence against women that is holistic, and creative, and results in local and global initiatives. A theological perspective and approach of the cross opens our imaginations to a myriad of ways to intervene in women's and children's lives and provide hope for futures free of violence. Education is an important tool for raising the consciousness of our churches to the plight of gendercide. However, education alone points to a moral approach and a partial response. A theology of the cross provides us with a perspective that is broad and that engages the language of the cross, theological understanding of the roles of suffering, human dignity, and the relationship of faith and ethics and spirituality within the context of community. The theology of the cross is the proclamation of the gospel that shapes our response to violence against women and girls. A theology of the cross frees us to minister and serve in the world, not as moral duty but because we have become free for the other as Christ is *pro me.*

This theological approach roots the Christian community in a confession of faith in Christ that has consequences. Dietrich Bonhoeffer and Eberhard Bethge offer contemporary reminders that worship and being church offer us a christocentric identity that requires a response to evil in the world. This theology does not seek a Christian society, nor does it require a reactionary agenda for the purpose of defending Christ in the world. Christ has broken into the world, and the Christian community is invited into faithful discipleship and the ministry of God in the world. We begin the work to end violence against women and girls not with political agendas and ideologies, not with educational programs and not with moral slogans, but in humility and prayer. As we worship, we obey the call to enter into Christ's work in the world to serve the poor, free the oppressed and care for our neighbors. There is a freedom that we encounter as we approach this creative work. We minister in obedience to Christ. However, salvation is not caught up in these good works. The cross and resurrection of Jesus provide us freedom, and the power of the cross in the world enables us to join in without concern for our success. The Christian church is called to be faithful, not successful.

The whole of the church is called to end gendercide. This is a confessional issue as defined by a theological approach of the cross. Violence committed against women and girls because of their gender is a sin against their humanity and dignity. Misogyny, domination and patriarchy are the roots of gendercide and the causes of the sin of idolatry. The community of God is called to care for and uphold the humanity of sex slaves, the girls who suffer genital mutilation, the battered women who have no place to go, the girls sent to orphanages because their parents can only take care of one son, and the young teen girls forced to marry at thirteen or fourteen. The violence is horrific, global, varied and pervasive, but it is all rooted in religious and cultural biases against women. Educational efforts are a necessary part of the response, but the Christian church needs to first confess that it has not shattered the silence that still exists around gendercide. It still needs to confess its collusion, both within the church and in the world, that maintains institutional and systemic violence. Many church communities have helpful educational programs that raise the consciousness of members, and many offer counseling referrals to battered women and sexual abuse survivors. Many more are engaged in a network of resources that ensure that women and children find a safe shelter and receive clothes, food and protection. Nevertheless, there is not a sustained, holistic response that condemns gendercide as a confessional issue and a call for the whole of the church to end systematic violence against women and girls. Our point of departure for a holistic response to ending violence against women and girls is Christ.

CHRISTIAN HOPE

The eschatological dimension of Christian discipleship includes an understanding of the true meaning of Christian hope. Historically, Christian hope has often been used as a means to preserve the status quo perpetuated by quietism. For example, during the civil rights movement, many well-meaning Christians cautioned Martin Luther King Jr. to be patient, not to demand equal rights for African Americans because change would come someday. They wrote in a letter to the editor that the civil rights leader's actions were "unwise and untimely." King responded to this perversion of Christian hope in his classic writing "A Letter from Birmingham Jail." James Washington writes in his introduction to the letter, "Dr. King wanted Christian ministers to see that the meaning of Christian discipleship was at the heart of the African American struggle for freedom, justice and equality."[1] Indeed, Dr. King attacked this false notion of Christian hope as a passive collusion with evil and violence and promoted a discipleship centered in action.

> In the midst of blatant injustices inflicted upon the Negro, I have watched white churches stand on the sideline and merely mouth pious irrelevancies and sanctimonious trivialities. In the midst of a mighty struggle to rid our nation of racial and economic injustice, I have heard so many ministers say, "Those are social issues with which the gospel has no real concern," and I have watched so many churches commit themselves to a completely otherworldly religion which made a strange dis-

---

[1]Martin Luther King Jr., "Letter from Birmingham City Jail (1963)," in *A Testament of Hope: The Essential Writings and Speeches of Dr. Martin Luther King, Jr.,* ed. James M. Washington (New York: HarperCollins, 1991), p. 289.

tinction between body and soul, the sacred and the secular. So here we are moving toward the exit of the twentieth century with a religious community largely adjusted to the status quo, standing as a taillight behind other community agencies rather than a headlight leading men to higher levels of justice.[2]

Christian hope rooted in the good news of the gospel proclaims the hope of the not yet—proclaims that the kingdom of God is yet to come in all its fullness *and* that the kingdom of God is here, in the now. Christian discipleship engages Christ in the poor, the hungry and the voiceless. Within the darkness and in the midst of violence and suffering, the Christian confesses Christ by way of service and serves by way of confession. Dietrich Bonhoeffer reminded us that both confession and action are necessary. Confessing Christ without "putting a spoke" in the wheel of institutions that support systemic violence is a dead religion. It is a religious practice that has nothing to do with the Jesus of the Scriptures.

To be called a Christian is not about being a passive receptor of God's grace. It is not a call to adhere to a type of detached confessionalism that has no concern for the world. A true Christian follows the Prince of Peace into the world. God encounters us and calls us to follow. A church that is not engaged in peacemaking, and justice building, and caring for whom Bonhoeffer identifies as the "farthest" is not the authentic church. Resistance to political, social and religious powers that seek to destroy the lives and dignity of women and girls is necessary to being a confessing community. Jesus' call to die to self in order to live is the great paradox of discipleship. Disciples of Christ have to lay down all plans, programs, identification with political figures, dreams, and even individual ideology and theology. At the cross, death to self lies in the hope of the person and work of Jesus Christ. But this hope exists not only in a kingdom yet to come but in the fulfilling of our call as peacemakers in this world.

---

[2]Ibid., p. 299.

COMMUNITY AND GLOBAL CONNECTEDNESS

The Christian church too often commits the sin of omission when it comes to justice making. The confession of these sins needs to lead us to turn toward a concern for our neighbor, for those who are exploited as a result of corporate greed, for the women and girl-children who are raped, sexually trafficked and violated, and for the vulnerable victims of wars. All those who call themselves disciples of Christ are called to recognize that an abandoned girl in China is their daughter, that a poor, hungry boy in Jamaica is their son. The homeless man in New York is their brother, and a woman grieving the loss of her child in Sudan, their sister. As Martin Luther King Jr. wrote so beautifully, "I cannot sit idly by in Atlanta and not be concerned about what happens in Birmingham. Injustice anywhere is a threat to justice everywhere. We are caught in an inescapable network of mutuality, tied in a single garment of destiny. Whatever affects one directly affects all indirectly."[3]

Discipleship is a call to be an advocate for those who cannot speak for themselves, and discipleship is a call to end injustice. Confession and resistance to injustice cannot be separated. Henri Nouwen, another twentieth-century spiritual writer and peacemaker, understood the relationship between Christian identity and justice making. He knew that in prayer we face a God who calls us out to bring peace, reconciliation and healing to a broken world.

> Christians should put survival of the planet ahead of national security, Henri once told an interviewer. Here is the mystery of our global responsibility: that we are in communion with Christ—and we are in communion with all people. . . . The fact that the people of Nicaragua, Guatemala, El Salvador, Russia, Afghanistan, and Ethiopia are our brothers and sisters is not obvious. People kill each other by the thousands and do not see themselves as brothers and sisters. If we want to be real peacemakers, national security cannot be our primary concern. Our primary concern should be survival of humanity, the survival of

---

[3]Ibid., p. 290.

the planet, and the health of all people. Whether we are Russians, Iraqis, Ethiopians, or North Americans, we belong to the same human family that God loves. And we have to start taking some risks—not just individually, but risks of a more global quality, risks to let other people develop their own independence, risks to share our wealth with others and invite refugees to our country, risks to offer sanctuary—because we are people of God.[4]

Violence against women and girls is not a singular problem. Global hunger, war, economic oppression, disease, political oppression, and social and religious practices all exacerbate and are connected to the violence. Interventions that reduce disease, end hunger and provide clean well water in poor communities and interventions that allow greater economic freedom can all help to reduce violence against women and girls. Nouwen offers a prophetic voice that cautions the church to discern the effect of national policies that impact the plight of those we are called to serve. When the state does not do enough to protect the vulnerable or interferes with their freedom and dignity, the church is called to speak truth to power, to aid victims and to actively resist political and economic powers that collude with evil practices.

All these twentieth-century theologians and activists underscored in their writings the importance of community as a necessary element of spirituality and a unifying dimension to justice making. Dorothy Day understood that the thousands that she fed in the Catholic Worker houses during the Depression were her brother and sisters. Nouwen taught that the poor in Africa and Asia and all over the world are our responsibility and that responsibility takes precedence over national security and economic interests. Martin Luther King Jr. argued that the enemy of the civil rights workers, the white racists, were children of God and that peaceful active nonviolence would not only bring about justice but win over their racist white brothers and sisters. In 1932,

---

[4]John Dear, "Introduction," in Henri Nouwen, *The Road to Peace: Writings on Peace and Justice*, ed. John Dear (Maryknoll, NY: Orbis, 2003), p. xxvi.

Dietrich Bonhoeffer wrote:

> The commandment to love is addressed to us Christians first of all in the
> sense that we ourselves have peace with every other person, as Christ
> did when he preached peace to his congregation, using the example of
> making peace with one's brother or with one's neighbor, or the example
> of the Good Samaritan. If we do not have this personal peace, we cannot
> preach peace to the nations [*Völker*]. And most people who are annoyed
> by hearing about peace among nations already question the love for
> one's personal enemies.[5]

THEOLOGICAL REFLECTION AND RESPONSE

Following a discussion or lecture on theological foundations for addressing violence against women and girls, I am frequently asked the following: "What do we do now? What are some activities and programs our church can implement to end the violence?" I am tempted to list "things to do." And in fact, there are many actions that aid in reducing local and global violence against women. In this chapter I describe a few of these actions that make a difference in the lives of women and girls. However, the objective of this book it to encourage the church to engage in broad theological reflection and to do the difficult work of examining Bonhoeffer's two questions to the church: Who is Jesus Christ for us today? What is the role of the church in the world today? Every generation needs to wrestle with these questions and, while rooted in the confession of faith, be shaped by the living Christ at work in the world. In terms of the work of ending violence against women and girls these questions will lead to other questions, some of which were posed in chapter one: What are the nature and roots of the violence? How is the violence that these women and girls experienced a symptom of larger cultural, spiritual and economic conditions in our churches and so-

---

[5]Dietrich Bonhoeffer, *Berlin: 1932–1933*, trans. Isabel Best and David Higgins, ed. Larry L. Rasmussen, vol. 12 of *Dietrich Bonhoeffer Works—English Edition* (Minneapolis: Fortress, 2009), p. 260.

ciety? How do we respond as a *whole* church community? What do Scripture and our confession of faith teach us regarding an approach toward violence and peacemaking? What concepts, language and orientation does our theology offer to help us shape a cohesive, powerful response to the violence? How is the violence in our local community related to violence against women and girls experienced globally? Should we define this as a confessional, broad issue needing a multifaceted approach rather than defining this merely as a moral issue that is worthy only of being relegated to a small group of interested community members? How does our confession of faith lead us to be actively involved in resisting institutional violence and promote just social policies?

Theologians of the cross will respond to the evil of gendercide by naming it as sin and renouncing all forms of violence against women and girls as opposed to the Christian confession of faith and Scripture. Discipleship means following Christ, not programs. From this perspective, the whole of the church needs to engage in living out hope-filled lives in service to our neighbors. Therefore, the following discussion on church and individual activities that help reduce violence against women and girls offers only partial remedies and should not be viewed as the church's starting point. The beginning of the work to end the violence, oppression and marginalization of women and girls is for the church to be the church! Confess Christ and follow Christ into the world. Resistance to religious, political and social policies that obstruct the gospel and lives of millions of women and girls begins in prayer, and in humility. There is a steep cost to being church. The true church renounces the illusion of power, identification with political ideologies, prideful self-righteous claims on church strategies for instituting a Christian society, efforts on raising church attendance and being culturally relevant, substituting ethics for doctrine and the confession of faith, and being a comfortable self-serving institution. Our confession of faith reminds us who God is and challenges us to move beyond confession to activism.

From a perspective of the cross, the whole of the church can engage in a myriad of efforts to counter gendercide, some of which include consciousness raising; a prophetic call to end violence; support of political, social and religious efforts to end violence against women and girls; aid to victims; and political resistance to systemic institutional supports of ongoing violence. Dietrich Bonhoeffer's three approaches of the church to the state (as described in the previous chapter) offer a helpful framework for considering the response of the church today in relation to gendercide. The following are some possible ways of engaging in the work to end the violence. However, through theological reflection and prayer, individual church communities, denominations and churches working on an interdenominational level can decide creatively on a multifaceted approach for a whole church response. The incarnational response allows for churches to frame their response creatively in partnership with non-Christian religious organizations, secular organizations and individual experts in the field of violence against women.

THE PROPHETIC VOICE: SPEAKING UP FOR THE VOICELESS

I always feel honored to hear the stories from women and girls of their experiences of suffering, pain and, sometimes, torment. I am also always impressed by the survival skills of these women and girls and by how they manage to somehow continue to function and move within their worlds while silently hiding their pain, fear and shame. We often refer to those who have been battered and sexually abused as victims. However, in my experience, these women and girls are valiant survivors. They are resourceful, and many of the survivors carry, by their own sheer will, tremendous burdens and suffering. Yet, many struggle to voice their pain. I counseled one young woman for two years before she was psychologically able to tell me how her boyfriend played Russian roulette with a loaded gun to her head and raped her repeatedly at gunpoint. She had relayed horrific violence over those two years, but her feelings of shame silenced the sexual violence she experienced. She had grown up in a middle-class Christian home and could not conceive of how her community would accept her if they knew about her victimization. Many young teens and women do not share with their Christian parents their experiences of violence and rape for fear that they will not be believed or will be judged. Unfortunately, many girls and women have come forward to pastors, parents and other church leaders and have been silenced or convinced that it will not happen again and, therefore, told that there is no need to speak further of "the incident."

In its silence regarding abuse and in its silencing of the survivors of violence, the church has colluded with the perpetrators. For every survivor silenced, there is a perpetrator of violence that has been supported in their sin and crime of violence. Violence remains a part of the political and cultural fabric in the lives of too many women and children. One pastor's wife discussed the physical battering she had endured for years at the hands of her husband. When she shared her experience with the elders, they did not believe her. How could a popular and charismatic pastor of a large congregation perpetrate such evil on his wife? How did they not know about it? He was not the "type" to abuse his partner. Soon after her report, they found out that he was having an extramarital affair. For this reason they fired him from the pastorate. The pastor's wife felt betrayed by her church for their indifference to her pain and the lack of response and support. One survivor reported to me that her church leaders did not believe her reports of abuse. They responded, "He is such a great worship leader!" Years ago, as a result of hearing so many stories of this type, I decided to offer training to pastors on the issue of domestic violence and strategies for church responses. Many pastors admitted their collusion with the perpetrators by their silence and lack of action.

Silencing survivors of violence is only one facet of this problem. We can also collude with perpetrators by not holding them accountable for their abuse. The language of the cross calls a thing what it is. Abuse against women and girls is sin. It is a crime and a human rights issue.

Cooperating with and working with law enforcement and programs that hold perpetrators of violence accountable are necessary endeavors to ensure the safety of women and girls in our communities. After speaking at one conference on domestic violence, a woman shared that her pastor told her not to offer testimony against her abusive husband. He believed that the church should not allow law enforcement into their community. This form of silence is harmful not only to the victim of the abuse but to the whole of the community. An incarnational theology shapes an ecclesiology that engages the church to work within the wider community. Secular authority and experts can act as partners in helping to end the violence. Christ works through Christian and non-Christian resources.

The church is called to be a prophetic voice that speaks truth to power. Harmful economic and political policies that do not allow for needed resources for women and their families are a hindrance for women's ability to become independent and provide for their families. Laws that exclude women and children from needed shelter and other resources because of their immigrant status endanger their lives. The church is called to be a prophetic voice for all those who have no voice within the state. It is important for the Christian community to become educated with regard to the availability of resources for all battered women and children and to work to ensure the provision of fair policies for the poor and marginalized in our society. Government policies and laws in other countries that do not provide for the protection of women and children are part of the institutional web of evil that maintains harmful practices such as the one-child policy in China and genital mutilation in many African countries. The voice of the American church and global church can work together to denounce harmful practices and to educate and empower women to resist such practices. Dietrich Bonhoeffer's first suggestion for church action is the call to the church to speak for the voiceless, speak truth to power and confess our faith, which renounces idolatry and hatred, in order to resist systematic violence.

AID TO SURVIVORS

It is not enough to speak against injustice and for the safety of survivors of violence. Bonhoeffer's second call for church action involves tangible help for victims. Our confession of faith rooted in the cross frees us to come alongside those who have experienced violence and provide them with the resources necessary for healing, restoration and lives free of abuse. This action of aid is in most churches' comfort zone. Those churches that are open to acknowledging the existence of violence in women and girls' lives are usually generous in their financial, spiritual and emotional support. Battered women programs rely on the support of churches to supply resources for victims. In some communities churches have developed direct relationships with battered women's shelters, transitional housing programs, food pantries and other economic resources that women and children depend upon while fleeing violent situations. Referrals to counseling and legal advocacy are other important resources that churches can and often do provide.

Local aid is important and necessary for women and their children to be able to survive in safety. More resources are always needed, especially in rural and poorer communities. It is also important for churches to engage in local *and* global initiatives to provide for women and their children. One such global initiative that has shown promising inroads to reducing violence against women and children is an economic initiative called *microfinance*. Microfinance, that is, the provision of financial support to small businesses run by very poor clients primarily in low-income countries, provides opportunities to individuals and families that otherwise would have no ability to secure funding for family businesses. This activity is very valuable for several reasons. Churches can easily become involved in a short amount of time. There are several microfinance organizations that can be easily accessed, and they direct funds quickly to poor women wanting to start up small businesses. Microfinance organizations are global, and as churches become involved in microfinancing, they also become educated about the plight of millions of hungry and poor women and children around the world. It is also a personal way for church groups to become involved. As members commit funds to a woman, they become familiar with her story and can follow on the microfinance website how she progresses in the development of her small business. These small businesses mean the difference between life and death for many women and their families, and help to reduce violence in their families and communities.

Survivor aid/global interventions. Violence against women and girls is not an isolated problem. Economic conditions, access to health care, social and cultural norms, and religious beliefs all play a part in the existence and ongoing problem of gendercide. The hopeful news is that there are many intervention strategies that offer a wide array of possibilities for reducing the violence. The story of intervention by a Christian organization in Lebanon, as described in chapter one, provides an illustration of how economic empowerment stopped the transport of several young women into sexual slavery in the Middle East. Their provision of jobs in a small business that makes soap offered an alternative to working in brothels to support the women's families at home. An intervention anywhere in the area of women's health and education, and in the area of economic development, can make a significant difference in the lives of millions of women. Microfinance is one strategy that has been shown to be effective in reducing violence against women and girls.

Women and children are more vulnerable to poverty because they may have less access to financial help; therefore, they are caught in a web of poverty that can exacerbate a lack of access to health care. One in five people worldwide survives on less than $1.25 a day,[6] and the majority of those are children and women. Women and children are caught in a web of hunger, poverty, disease and violence with no hope of escape. A lack of resources makes it nearly impossible for millions of women to

---

[6]"Introducing World Vision Micro," *World Vision,* accessed July 12, 2013, www.worldvisionmicro.org /downloads/micro/landing/event_kits/pastor_talking_points.pdf.

escape violence that may be culturally acceptable in their families. One Brazilian woman reported that in her community domestic violence was so prevalent and poverty was so epidemic that women could not conceive of another type of life for their daughters. Anti-poverty programs offer some hope of providing possible alternatives to remaining in abusive homes.

Approximately fourteen million of the world's poorest women have access to financial services through microfinance institutions (MFIs), nongovernmental organizations (NGOs), banks and other financial institutions.[7] Women account for three-fourths of those being served by these services. These institutions have been very creative in developing products and services that allow access for women who have traditionally been denied loans from formal financial services.[8] Microfinance organizations work with field partners in the countries they serve. These field partners screen borrowers, post loan requests, distribute the loans, provide administration services and collect repayments.[9] For example, Kiva, a well-known microfinance organization, has 204 field partners in 69 countries. The number of Kiva users is approximately 1,446,975. These clients have received an average loan of $407.[10] For many, small loans for starting businesses are the difference between a life free of violence and hunger for their children and a life of early death, disease and desperation.

Sarah began her business cooking doughnuts on a cement slab in front of her home. Whenever it rained, she would have to shut down her small business. With loans from World Vision she was able to expand her business. She also employs five other persons from her community. Sarah remembers her life as a child as very different from the life she is now able to give her children. She only ate one meal a day

---

[7]Susy Cheston and Lisa Kuhn, "Empowering Women Through Microfinance," in *Pathways Out of Poverty: Innovations in Microfinance for the Poorest Families*, ed. Sam Daley-Harris (Bloomfield, CT: Kumarian Press, 2002), p. 173.

[8]Ibid.

[9] Kiva, "Our Field Partners," accessed July 12, 2013, www.kiva.org/partners.

[10] Kiva, "Statistics," accessed July 14, 2013, www.kiva.org/about/stats.

and was not able to attend much school because her mother could not afford the school fees. She reports that after receiving her loan and expanding the business her children are well fed, attend school and have hope for the future.[11]

Some studies over the past ten years have shown that MFIs are providing a decreased percentage of loans to women and that average loans to women are smaller than men's. This may be a result of greater poverty among women and a greater difficulty for women's businesses to utilize the capital.[12] Programs that consist of giving financial help solely to women may create tension and conflict within the household as women are empowered to become more financially independent from their husbands. In addition, the leaders of most MFIs are men. Women's involvement on the boards of directors; shaping the vision, products and services; and implementing the services is mostly missing.[13] There are now many studies that indicate that programs that provide financial resources for small businesses run only by poor women are not enough to reduce violence against women. The most successful programs are those that also provide health education, supportive alternatives to remaining in violent relationships, and efforts to alter community and cultural norms and attitudes regarding the acceptance of family violence.

Microfinance programs have the potential to encourage and enable women to become more independent as the relationship between the provider and the client is "inherently empowering."[14] Several studies indicate that microfinance improves not only women's financial situations but their self-confidence and their ability to make decisions that benefit their families. This improvement in self-confidence and esteem is important when considering strategies in reducing violence. Poor men may feel as powerless as poor women, but cultural, religious and social norms often support their dominance within patriarchal families. Self-confidence

---

[11]"Sarah's Story," *World Vision*, accessed July 12, 2013, www.worldvisionmicro.org/success_stories/6.
[12]Cheston and Kuhn, "Empowering Women Through Microfinance," p. 171.
[13]Ibid.
[14]Ibid.

and access to better health care, education and financial independence provide more alternatives for abused women in violent situations.

This is true for women everywhere. During a group session I conducted for battered women, Julie reported that she had no alternative but to stay with her abusive husband. One woman in the group inquired why she felt that she could not get a job and support herself. Julie replied that her husband repeatedly told her she was too stupid to be able to work and that she did not have the ability to keep a checkbook. Another woman gently asked her what work she did before marrying. Julie replied, "I was an accountant!" The silence that followed was palpable. During the rest of that group session the women encouraged Julie to consider her own abilities to be independent. Julie slowly began to realize that her husband had used very effective strategies of psychological and economic abuse over a period of years. It took months, but with group support Julie became more confident and eventually secured a job and left her abusive husband. This group met in an affluent suburban setting in the United States. Julie first needed the self-confidence and support to remember who she was and her abilities and skills. Increased self-esteem ultimately led her to find a safe place for herself and her children and a job that offered her financial security. In other areas of the world, women do not have the opportunities to access financial help that enables them to work, to build self-confidence and respect within their communities, and to seek opportunities to live free from violence. Financial support by way of microfinance organizations allows women not only these opportunities but psychological and social support as well.

An increase in self-confidence and financial independence does not necessarily translate to the breaking up of families. Many studies indicate that families become more stabilized, the additional family income provides for less stress in the family, husbands increase their respect for their wives, and the children have better access to health care and educational systems.[15] The Women's Empowerment Program in Nepal conducted a

---

[15]Ibid., p. 189.

study that showed that an average of 89,000 out of 130,000 or 68 percent of women in its program experienced an increase in their decision-making roles in the areas of buying and selling property, sending their daughters to school and health care for their families. A World Relief partner in Rwanda found that 54 percent of clients experienced an increase in their ability to control or influence business decisions, and 38 percent experienced an increase in decision making in their families, 38 percent in their communities and 54 percent in their churches.[16]

Studies have found fewer incidents of violence against women among women who are clients of microfinance organizations. The fear of public exposure and women's financial contribution to the household reduced family violence.[17] The Working Women's Forum found that almost 50 percent of its members who had experienced familial violence were able to stop it through group and personal empowerment. Also in areas where marriage at a young age is expected, financial independence provided an avenue for freedom from abusive homes.[18] A 2004 report by members of the Consultative Group to Assist the Poor (CGAP) notes that increased contributions of resources to the home led to increased self-esteem and declining levels of violence for clients in Bangladesh. They surveyed 130 households and found that women with loans were less likely to be beaten. The report also noted that clients in Bolivia and Ghana experienced increased self-confidence and improved status within their communities.[19]

A study evaluating the IMAGE (Intervention with Microfinance for AIDS and Gender Equity) intervention program in rural South Africa concluded that this program was effective in reducing violence against women. The IMAGE intervention combined a microfinance program with participatory training to understand HIV infection,

---

[16]Ibid., p. 185.

[17]Ibid., p. 189.

[18]Ibid., p. 190.

[19]Nishita, "Microfinance and Violence Against Women," *Kiva Fellows Blog: Stories from the Field,* posted April 27, 2010, http://fellowsblog.kiva.org/2010/04/27/microfinance-and-violence-against -women/.

gender norms, domestic violence and sexuality. Outcome measures included past years' experience of intimate partner violence and nine indicators of women's empowerment. Qualitative data about changes occurring within intimate relationships, loan groups and the community were also collected. The study concluded that the past year's risk of physical or sexual violence by an intimate partner was reduced by more than half. Improvement in women's empowerment was observed. Women were at less risk of violence because they challenged the acceptability of violence, increased expectations of better treatment from partners and left abusive relationships. Public awareness of violence against women and children within these communities also helped to decrease the violence. The conclusion indicated that economic and social empowerment of women contributes to a reduction in intimate partner violence.[20]

Summary. Microfinance has the potential to significantly change women's lives. Financial independence may initiate a number of changes that ultimately will allow women to gain greater respect in their families and in their communities and prevent violence in the home. It also may provide a way to gain resources to enable women to leave situations that are harmful to themselves and their children. Microfinance is not the only answer, but it is one resource that has an impact on the women and girls who otherwise would be exploited and possibly abused.

There are limitations to these programs. Financing for small businesses alone will not end the horror of gendercide, but the best of these programs, combined with health information and education for girls, are an important resource in the work to end gendercide. Networking, leadership training, self-management and support are also elements of these programs that are helpful to women as they offer the skills and hope for new lives for their families. The most effective programs are those that take a holistic approach by considering the cultural, political,

---

[20]Julia C. Kim et al., "Understanding the Impact of a Microfinance-Based Intervention on Women's Empowerment and the Reduction of Intimate Partner Violence in the IMAGE Study, South Africa," *American Journal of Public Health* 97 (2007): 1794–1802, www.ncbi.nlm.nih.gov/pmc/articles/PMC1994170.

religious and social environments of the women that are receiving the benefits of these programs.[21]

If every Christian church spent two adult education hours becoming informed about these resources and tools, what a difference it might make in the lives of thousands of women and girls! Microfinancing is a useful tool for both individuals and churches in their efforts to make a difference in the lives of impoverished families. Local churches can gather a group of families together, select a microfinance organization, commit to giving a certain dollar amount and empower many poor women in Africa, Asia, South Asia or anywhere else in the world. Participating in a microfinancing project also offers an opportunity to learn about the lives of these women and children and to follow their success as they develop their businesses. It is a local effort that has great global possibilities for women and their families.

Aid to survivors of violence is a necessary component of a church response to gendercide. Providing resources through the church and existing community agencies greatly benefits women on the local level. Through theological reflection and whole-church discussion, strategies for global intervention can be explored. Microfinance is just one possible strategy for empowering and equipping women for alternative lives free from violence. NGOs and other organizations that provide education for girls, health information, clean water through the building of community wells, local clinics and other global initiatives are all important avenues for effecting change that reduces gendercide. Supporting educational programs and church policies that provide biblical teaching on the dignity and equality of women and girls can help to place women in positions where their gifts are utilized. Local and global church teaching that prevents women from providing leadership in their Christian communities supports a religious culture that denigrates women and girls based on their gender. The inclusion of women in church leadership enriches the whole of the church and has Christ as the starting point for mission instead of political ideologies based on false biblical teaching.

---

[21]Cheston and Kuhn, "Empowering Women Through Microfinance," p. 217.

CHURCH RESISTANCE

Dietrich Bonhoeffer's third suggestion for church intervention involves church resistance. The move from speaking for the voiceless and aiding survivors of violence to resisting evil institutional and political supports is more difficult for the Christian church. It requires a commitment to theological reflection and discussion and the willingness to enter into uncomfortable engagement in the larger social, cultural and political arena. When questioned why a forum was to take place regarding concerns about the involvement of the church with certain financial institutions (this was perceived to be political and possibly divisive for the church) the pastor remarked, "It's also political to be passive and not to be intentional about how we manage our money." It is often seen as divisive, dangerous in fact, to engage in social policy discussions within our church communities. In fact, the pastor was right. *Not* engaging in discussions is also political. Churches that stood by and did not work to end slavery, promote equality during the civil rights movement, or work to save the Jews and others from certain death were also acting politically. Passivity in the face of evil and the promotion of violence toward others constitute a political act of collusion.

Political action and engagement in social change within the perspective of a theology of the cross are often not viewed as the essence of Jesus' mission. They are not seen as salvific, and they are not working toward a Christian society. However, theologians of the cross pursue justice in the penultimate realm of the world because the church is Christ in the world. There is no optimistic, utopian hope for a kingdom of God on earth. There is only the Christ that encounters us and calls us to be *for the other.* There are limits to state power and limits to the role of the church within the state. However, a church of the cross, rooted in the confession of faith, recognizes and responds to evil. There are consequences to being people of God engaged in the world that God created and loves. This may, in certain circumstances, mean political engagement and resistance to institutions that promote violence. In the area of violence against women and girls, there are cultural, religious and political systems that continue to promote gendercide. This is the reality. Do we recognize those systems, and do we work to promote justice though it may mean political resistance and engagement? Answering this question requires theological reflection, discussion and willingness to identify with the survivors of violence.

BANGLADESH: AN OPPORTUNITY FOR LOCAL/GLOBAL RESISTANCE

In the first chapter I described the connections between violence against women and girls and all other social and political issues, including poverty, disease and the lack of economic opportunities. The following story offers one example of how church communities can act to end economic injustice in one corner of the world and at the same time reduce global violence against women and girls. Local initiatives such as letter-writing campaigns, boycotts, acting consciously about the way we consume goods and reducing materialism should be born out of intentional theological reflection on Christ. These local initiatives can have a strategic impact on the health and welfare of women and girls worldwide.

Tahmina Akhter Sadia began working in the garment factory at eleven years old. Four years later, on April 24, 2013, she refused to enter the Rana Plaza factory, located outside of Dhaka, Bangladesh. She had noticed the cracks in the wall and felt the shudder of the building. Some workers had fled the day before in fear for their lives. Tahmina's supervisor slapped her in the face and forced her to work. A few hours later the building collapsed. Fortunately, Tahmina survived, but over eleven hundred other workers did not.

Most of the over four million garment workers in five thousand factories in Bangladesh are women and girls. Nineteen-year-old Parveen Akter's story is typical. She worked for three years and supported her family of nine, who lived 150 miles away in the rural district of Pabna. They relied on her income for their survival. With overtime, Parveen earned $102 monthly. Parveen did not survive the collapse of the Rana

Plaza factory. Her family reported that they do not know what they will do to survive.[22]

The ready-made garments (RMG) industry makes up more than 75 percent of Bangladesh's export income and is the largest employer of women and girls. Bangladesh is second only to China as the world's largest exporter of clothing. RMG jobs offer an alternative to farm jobs and jobs as domestic servants. RMG jobs offer a higher wage and often support large extended families. These jobs have actually helped elevate the social status of women and reduced the number of forced marriages in some rural communities.

The problem lies with the continuously dangerous conditions in many Asian factories. Most factory workers are powerless to change these conditions and are obligated to accept poor treatment by factory owners. If they complain about the conditions, they fear losing their jobs. Many women report physical and verbal abuse by factory supervisors if they do not meet their quotas. Reports by women factory workers describe long hours and almost intolerable conditions. Foreign buyers never see the horrific conditions when inspecting these factories. Owners are careful to clean up on those days and present a very different image from the reality of women's and girls' lives.[23]

Some United States retailers have tried to improve conditions, but there isn't any pressure on American corporations to stop doing business abroad or to ensure better working conditions for these factories. Many European retailers have signed agreements to improve conditions, and a few United States retailers have also indicated that they will invest in improvements. However, more government oversight and pressure on corporations are needed to ensure better working conditions and to create a culture of intolerance for abuse toward the

---

[22]Holly Williams, "Survivor of Bangladesh Factory Collapse Speaks Out," *CBS News*, May 23, 2013, www.cbsnews.com/8301-18563_162-57586001/survivor-of-bangladesh-factory-collapse-speaks-out/.

[23]Sohel Uddin, "Bangladesh Factory Collapse: Why Women Endure Danger to Make Clothes for the West," *NBC News*, May 26, 2013, http://worldnews.nbcnews.com/_news/2013/05/26/18447688-bangladesh-factory-collapse-why-women-endure-danger-to-make-clothes-for-the-west?lite.

workers in order to protect poor girls and women.[24]

What can churches do to offer resistance to this type of global violence against women and girls? We live in a consumer-driven culture. How do we change the culture in our own communities to prompt a theologically thoughtful response to materialism? How can churches economically support the work of women and girls in Asia and yet not collude with the corporations and owners who support violence? Possibilities include supporting companies that invest in safe factories and offer good wages by buying their products; educating members regarding companies that refuse to provide safe working conditions; boycotting those stores and products that refuse to support workers; writing letters to companies and requesting that they only purchase their products from safe factories in Asia; and pressuring our government to ensure that United States companies abide by safety codes and fair wage practices both within and outside of our borders. These are only a few actions for churches to consider. Action starts with theological reflection on our point of departure: Christ. Speaking about injustice and speaking for the voiceless are critical. Aiding victims is critical. Resistance to unjust systems and institutions is the most difficult step, but is also a critical step to create change.

Let us establish in our church communities "the mind of Christ" (1 Cor 2:16). We need to be aware of how our cultures and society influence our thinking regarding our view of injustice. As church communities, do we humble ourselves before the cross and confess our sins of omission and silence in the face of violence? Do we identify with the poor and oppressed as Jesus did, or do we build walls of comfort around us? Does our freedom in Christ manifest itself as freedom to serve others? Do we speak truth to power? Do we proclaim the gospel knowing that it may have political and social-policy implications? Or are we captive to political ideologies that make it difficult for us to be captive to the word of God? Do we name sin and

---

[24]Anna McMullen, "Bangladesh Factory Collapse: Who Really Pays for Our Cheap Clothes?," *CNN*, April 26, 2013, www.cnn.com/2013/04/25/opinion/bangladesh-factory-collapse-opinion/.

hold perpetrators of violence accountable? Are we open to using the tools offered by human rights organizations as tools for change in the legal realm? Are we committed to ending denial, the minimization of violence and victim blaming?

CONCLUSION

Jesus' proclamation of his mission as the One who came to give "good news to the poor . . . to proclaim release to the captives and recovery of sight to the blind, to let the oppressed go free" (Lk 4:18) is manifested through his birth into a poor family in an occupied country without a bed for the night. It is woven into every story that he told, every healing touch and gesture. He carried it with him to everyone to whom he spoke no matter what their status within their community. His desire to free those who are oppressed, liberate the captives and heal broken bodies, minds and spirits is evident in every place he walked, to every person he touched. To his very last breath his mission was lived out in love. From the cradle to the cross his body held the good news of life and liberation for any and all he encountered.

The theology of the cross is a deeply incarnational theology of the body. There is no room for a disembodied spirituality in the life of Jesus. He carried his mission out in the most physical manner within the social and political reality of his community. He gathered the children to himself; he dared to speak to a foreign woman alone and saved an adulteress from sure death. He allowed a bleeding woman to touch him and fed a hungry crowd. He cared not for laws that prevented him from healing on the holy Sabbath, and he welcomed a woman who dared to touch his body while she washed his feet. He directed his anger toward those who sought to put the law and reason above human dignity and love. At the cross he suffered excruciating pain and yet remembered to secure care for his mother and to offer forgiveness to a criminal. The heart of the theology of the cross is the radical encounter with the living Christ who calls us to enter into relationship with the suffering, oppressed and marginalized.

The time for ministering to abused women and girls is now. The time to work for structural change that will improve the lives of women and girls is now. The time to speak on behalf of those who cannot speak for themselves because of oppressive systems that deny their human dignity is now. Gendercide is a confessional issue. The body of the living Christ, the authentic church, enters into the world, speaks truth to power and resists social, religious and political structures that continue to support violence against women and girls. Jesus proclaimed his mission as one of freedom and healing. Within this proclamation we find Jesus' demand to "Come, follow me."

BIBLIOGRAPHY

Adams, Carol J. *Woman-Battering*. Minneapolis: Fortress, 1994.

Amnesty International. *It's About Time! Human Rights Are Women's Rights*. New York: Amnesty International USA, 1995.

Aubert, Annette G. "Theodicy and the Cross and the Theology of Dietrich Bonhoeffer." *Trinity Journal* 32 NS (2011): 47-67.

Augustine. *City of God*. Translated by Marcus Dods. New York: Modern Library Classics, 1993.

Babu, Chaya. "285 Indian Girls Shed 'Unwanted' Names." *Guardian*, October 22, 2011. www.guardian.co.uk/world/feedarticle/9908439.

Benne, Robert. "The Lutheran Tradition and Public Theology." *Lutheran Theological Seminary Bulletin* 76 (1995): 15-26.

Bernardin, Joseph. "A Consistent Ethic of Life: An American-Catholic Dialogue." Gannon Lecture, Fordham University, December 6, 1983. www.hnp.org /publications/ hnpfocus/BConsistentEthic1983.pdf.

Bethge, Eberhard. *Friendship and Resistance: Essays on Dietrich Bonhoeffer*. Grand Rapids: Eerdmans, 1995.

———. *Dietrich Bonhoeffer: A Biography*. Edited by Victoria J. Barnett. Rev. ed. Minneapolis: Fortress, 2000.

Bograd, Michele. "Feminist Perspectives on Wife Abuse: An Introduction." In *Feminist Perspectives on Wife Abuse*, edited by Yllö and Bograd, pp. 11-26.

Bonhoeffer, Dietrich. *Berlin: 1932-1933*. Translated by Isabel Best and David Higgins. Edited by Larry L. Rasmussen. Vol. 12 of *Dietrich Bonhoeffer Works—English Edition*. Minneapolis: Fortress, 2009.

———. *Conspiracy and Imprisonment: 1940–1945*. Translated by Isabel Best and

David Higgins. Edited by Larry L. Rasmussen. Vol. 12 of *Dietrich Bonhoeffer Works—English Edition*. Minneapolis: Fortress, 2006.

———. *Creation and Fall*. New York: Touchstone Books, 1997.

———. *Dietrich Bonhoeffer: Witness to Jesus Christ*. Edited by John W. de Gruchy. Minneapolis: Fortress, 1987.

———. *Dietrich Bonhoeffer Works—English Edition*. 16 vols. Minneapolis: Fortress, 2003–2013.

———. *Discipleship*. Translated by Reinhard Krauss and Barbara Green. Edited by John D. Godsey and Geoffrey B. Kelly. Vol. 4 of *Dietrich Bonhoeffer Works— English Edition*. Minneapolis: Fortress, 2003.

———. *Ethics*. Translated by Reinhard Krauss, Charles C. West and Douglas W. Stott. Edited by Clifford J. Green. Vol. 6 of *Dietrich Bonhoeffer Works— English Edition*. Minneapolis: Fortress, 2003.

———. *Letters and Papers from Prison*. Edited by Eberhard Bethge. New York: Collier Books, 1971.

———. *No Rusty Swords: Letters, Lectures and Notes 1928–1936*. In *The Collected Works of Dietrich Bonhoeffer*. Translated by Edwin H. Robertson and John Bowdon. Saint James Place, London: Collins, Sons & Co., 1965.

———. *A Testament to Freedom: The Essential Writings of Dietrich Bonhoeffer*. Edited by Geoffrey B. Kelly and F. Burton Nelson. New York: HarperCollins, 1995.

———. *Who Is Christ for Us?* Edited and translated by Craig L. Nessan. Minneapolis: Fortress, 2002.

Cheston, Susy, and Lisa Kuhn. "Empowering Women Through Microfinance." In *Pathways out of Poverty: Innovations in Microfinance for the Poorest Families*, edited by Sam Daley-Harris, pp. 167-228. Bloomfield, CT: Kumarian Press, 2002.

"Children Go Home as China Cracks Trafficking Ring." *Reuters-Africa*, January 3, 2008. Adapted by Humantrafficking.org. www.humantrafficking.org /updates/827.

"China Human Rights Fact Sheet." Robert F. Kennedy Memorial Center for Human Rights. March 1995. www.christusrex.org/www1/sdc/hr_facts. html#Woman.

Cline, Elizabeth L. *Overdressed: The Shockingly High Cost of Cheap Fashion*. New York: Penguin Group, 2012.

Cook, Rebecca J., ed. *Human Rights of Women: National and International Perspectives*. Philadelphia: University of Pennsylvania Press, 1994.

Cooper-White, Pamela. *The Cry of Tamar: Violence Against Women and the Church Response*. Minneapolis: Fortress, 1995.

Cuthbert, Carrie, Mala Rafik and Kim Slote. "Letter to Sara K. Gould, Vice President for Program, Ms. Foundation for Women." January 30, 1998. New York. Private collection.

Dempster, Carolyn. "Rape—Silent War on South African Women." *BBC News*, April 9, 2002. http://news.bbc.co.uk/2/hi/1909220.stm.

Domestic Violence Facts. National Coalition Against Domestic Violence, 2007. www.ncadv.org/files/DomesticViolenceFactSheet(National).pdf.

Dramm, Sabine. *Dietrich Bonhoeffer: An Introduction to His Thought*. Peabody, MA: Hendrickson, 2007.

Ebeling, Gerhard. *Luther: An Introduction to His Thought*. Translated by R. A. Wilson. Philadelphia: Fortress, 1970.

Evans, Karin. *The Lost Daughters of China*. New York: Penguin Putnam, 2000.

Fact Sheet No. 23, Harmful Traditional Practices Affecting the Health of Women and Children. Geneva: Office of the High Commissioner for Human Rights, 2004.

Fontanarosa, Phil B. "The Unrelenting Epidemic of Violence in America: Truths and Consequences." *Journal of the American Medicine Association* 273 (1995): 1792-93.

Forde, Gerhard O. *On Being a Theologian of the Cross: Reflections on Luther's Heidelberg Disputation, 1518*. Grand Rapids: Eerdmans, 1997.

―――. "On Being a Theologian of the Cross." *Christian Century*, October 22, 1997, pp. 947-49. www.religion-online.org/showarticle.asp?title=320.

―――. *Theology Is for Proclamation*. Minneapolis: Fortress, 1990.

Forell, George W. *The Christian Lifestyle: Reflections on Romans 12–15*. Philadelphia: Fortress, 1975.

―――. *Faith Active in Love: An Investigation of the Principles Underlying Luther's Social Ethics*. New York: American Press, 1954.

―――. *The Proclamation of the Gospel in a Pluralistic World: Essays on Christianity and Culture*. Philadelphia: Fortress, 1973.

Forell, George W., and William H. Lazareth, eds. *Human Rights: Rhetoric or Reality*. Philadelphia: Fortress, 1978.

Foundation for AIDS Research. "Statistics: Women and HIV/AIDS." www.amfar
.org/About-HIV-and-AIDS/Facts-and-Stats/Statistics--Women-and-
HIV-AIDS/.

Friedman, Elisabeth. "Women's Human Rights: The Emergence of a Movement."
In *Women's Rights: Human Rights*, edited by Peters and Wolper, pp. 18-35.

"General Recommendation No. 19: General Comments and Recommendations of
the UN Treaty Bodies." Committee on the Elimination of Discrimination
Against Women. New York: United Nations, 1992. www.un.org/womenwatch
/daw/cedaw/recommendations/recomm.htm.

George, Timothy. *Theology of the Reformers*. Nashville: Broadman, 1988.

Green, Clifford, ed. *Karl Barth: Theologian of Freedom*. Minneapolis: Fortress, 1989.

Groves, Betsy McAlister. *Children Who See Too Much: Lessons from the Child
Witness to Violence Project*. Boston: Beacon, 2002.

Gruchy, John W. de, "The Development of Bonhoeffer's Theology." In Bonhoeffer,
Dietrich Bonhoeffer: Witness to Jesus Christ, pp. 1-42.

Harvard Humanitarian Initiative. "Congo-Kinshasa: New Report Shows Shocking
Pattern of Rape in Eastern Congo." *Oxfam International*, April 15, 2010. www
.oxfam.org/en/pressroom/pressrelease/2010-04-15/new-report-shows-shocking
-pattern-rape-eastern-congo.

The Hunger Project. "Know Your World: Facts About Hunger and Poverty." www.thp
.org/learn_more/issues/know_your_world_facts_about_hunger_and_poverty.

John XXIII. "*Pacem in Terris:* Encyclical Letter of Pope John XXIII on Establishing
Universal Peace in Truth, Justice, Charity, and Liberty." Rome, April 11, 1963.
www.vatican.va/holy_father/john_xxiii/encyclicals/documents/hf_j-xxiii
_enc_11041963_pacem_en.html.

Johnson, Keith L., and Timothy Larsen, eds. *Bonhoeffer, Christ, and Culture*.
Downers Grove, IL: InterVarsity Press, 2013.

Kadel, Andrew. *Matrology: A Bibliography of Writings by Christian Women from the
First to the Fifteenth Centuries*. New York: Continuum, 1995.

Keating, Ted. "Catholic Social Teaching and the Universal Declaration on Human
Rights." *Catholic Peace Voice* 23, no. 213 (Spring/Summer 1998). Reprinted at
www.hrusa.org/advocacy/community-faith/catholic1.shtm.

Kim, Julia C., Charlotte H. Watts, James R. Hargreaves, Luceth X. Ndhlovu,
Godfrey Phetla, Linda A. Morison, Joanna Busza, John D. H. Porter and Paul

Pronyk. "Understanding the Impact of a Microfinance-Based Intervention on Women's Empowerment and the Reduction of Intimate Partner Violence in the IMAGE Study, South Africa." *American Journal of Public Health* 97 (2007): 1794-1802. www.ncbi.nlm.nih.gov/pmc/articles/ PMC1994170.

King, Martin Luther, Jr. "Letter from Birmingham City Jail (1963)." In *A Testament of Hope: The Essential Writings and Speeches of Dr. Martin Luther King, Jr.,* ed. James M. Washington, pp. 289-302. New York: HarperCollins, 1991.

Kirshenbaum, Gayle. "After Victory, Women's Human Rights Movement Takes Stock." *Ms. Magazine* 4, no. 2 (September/October 1993): 20.

Kiva. "Our Field Partners." www.kiva.org/partners.

———. "Statistics." www.kiva.org/about/stats.

Kristof, Nicholas D. "After Wars, Mass Rapes Persist." *New York Times*, May 20, 2009. www.nytimes.com/2009/05/21/opinion/21kristof.html.

Kristof, Nicholas, and Sheryl WuDunn. *Half the Sky: Turning Oppression into Opportunities for Women Worldwide.* New York: Knopf, 2009.

Kroeger, Catherine Clark, and James R. Beck, eds. *Healing the Hurting: Giving Hope & Help to Abused Women.* Grand Rapids: Baker Books, 1998.

———. *Women, Abuse, and the Bible: How Scripture Can Be Used to Hurt or Heal.* Grand Rapids: Baker Books, 1996.

Kroeger, Catherine Clark, and Nancy Nason-Clark. *No Place for Abuse: Biblical & Practical Resources to Counteract Domestic Violence.* Downers Grove, IL: InterVarsity Press, 2001.

Kroeger, Catherine Clark, Nancy Nason-Clark and Barbara Fisher-Townsend, eds. *Beyond Abuse in the Christian Home: Raising Voices for Change.* Eugene, OR: Wipf & Stock, 2008.

Krüsche, Gunter. "Human Rights in a Theological Perspective: A Contribution from the GDR." *Lutheran World* 24, no. 1 (1977): 59-65.

Lindberg, Carter. *Beyond Charity: Reformation Initiatives for the Poor.* Minneapolis: Augsburg Fortress, 1993.

———. "Do Lutherans Shout Justification but Whisper Sanctification?" *Lutheran Quarterly* 13 (1999): 1-20.

———. "Luther's Concept of Offering." *Dialog* 35 (fall 1996): 251-57.

———. "Theory and Practice: Reformation Models of Ministry as Resource for the Present." *Lutheran Quarterly* 27 (1975): 27-35.

Livingston, David J. *Healing Violent Men: A Model for Christian Communities*. Minneapolis: Fortress, 2002.

Lloyd, Genevieve. "Augustine and Aquinas." In *Feminist Theology: A Reader*, edited by Ann Loades and Karen Armstrong, pp. 90-98. Louisville: Westminster, 1990.

Lohse, Bernhard. *A Short History of Christian Doctrine: From the First Century to the Present*. Translated by F. Ernest Stoeffler. Philadelphia: Fortress, 1985.

Luther, Martin. *Luther's Works*. Edited by Jaroslav Pelikan (vols. 1-30) and Helmut T. Lehmann (vols. 31-55). St. Louis: Concordia, 1968–.

Malone, Mary T. *Women and Christianity*. 3 vols. Maryknoll, NY: Orbis Books, 2000–2003.

Martin, Del. *Battered Wives*. San Francisco: Glide, 1976.

McCurley, Foster R., and John H. Reumann. "Human Rights in the Law and Romans (Series A)." In *Human Rights: Rhetoric or Reality*, edited by George W. Forell and William H. Lazarethm, pp. 5-30. Philadelphia: Fortress, 1978.

McGrath, Alister E. *Luther's Theology of the Cross*. Oxford: Blackwell, 1985.

McMullen, Anna. "Bangladesh Factory Collapse: Who Really Pays for Our Cheap Clothes?" *CNN*, April 26, 2013. www.cnn.com/2013/04/25/opinion /bangladesh-factory-collapse-opinion/.

Melki, Camille E. "Women and Church History." Lecture handout, Northeastern Seminary, Rochester, NY, February 13, 2012.

Mertus, Julie. "Our Human Rights: A Manual for Women's Human Rights." Unpublished article distributed for comments at the Fourth UN World Conference for Women, Beijing, China, August 1995.

Miles, Al. *Domestic Violence: What Every Pastor Needs to Know*. Minneapolis: Fortress, 2000.

Mitchell, Eileen. *Plantations and Death Camps: Religion, Ideology, and Human Dignity*. Minneapolis: Fortress, 2009.

Moltmann, Jürgen. *Der gekreuzigte Gott: Das Kreuz Christi als Grund und Kritik christlicher Theologie*. Munich: Gütersloher Verlagshaus, 1981.

Nason-Clark, Nancy. *The Battered Wife: How Christians Confront Family Violence*. Louisville: John Knox, 1997.

Nason-Clark, Nancy, and Catherine Clark Kroeger. *Refuge from Abuse: Healing and Hope for Abused Christian Women*. Downers Grove, IL: InterVarsity Press, 2004.

NiCarthy, Ginny, Karen Merriam and Sandra Coffman. *Talking It Out: A Guide to*

Groups for Abused Women. Seattle: Seal Press, 1984.

Nishita. "Microfinance and Violence Against Women." Kiva Fellows Blog: Stories from the Field. April 27, 2010. http://fellowsblog.kiva.org/2010/04/27/micro finance-and-violence-against-women/.

Nouwen, Henri. *The Road to Peace: Writings on Peace and Justice*. Edited by John Dear. Maryknoll, NY: Orbis, 2003.

Obinna, Chioma. "Nigeria: Safe Motherhood—Need for Access to Quality Prenatal and Delivery Services." *Vanguard*, February 17, 2012. http://allafrica.com /stories/201202170824.html.

Okin, Susan Moller. *Justice, Gender, and the Family*. New York: Basic Books, 1989.

Paton, William. *The Church and the New Order*. London: Student Christian Movement Press, 1941.

Peters, Julie, and Andrea Wolper, eds. *Women's Rights: Human Rights*. New York: Routledge, 1995.

Prenter, Regin. *Luther's Theology of the Cross*. Philadelphia: Fortress, 1971.

"Rape: It's a War Crime." *Los Angeles Times*, August 13, 2009. http://articles .latimes.com/2009/aug/13/opinion/ed-rape13

Robertson, Edwin. *The Shame and the Sacrifice: The Life and Martyrdom of Dietrich Bonhoeffer*. New York: Collier Books, 1988.

Scharffenorth, Gerta. *Becoming Friends in Christ: The Relationship Between Man and Woman as Seen by Luther*. Geneva: Lutheran World Federation, 1983.

Schechter, Susan. *Women and Male Violence: The Visions and Struggles of the Battered Women's Movement*. Boston: South End Press, 1982.

Tjaden, Patricia, and Nancy Thoennes. *Extent, Nature and Consequences of Intimate Partner Violence: Findings from the National Violence Against Women Survey*. Washington, DC: US Department of Justice, Office of Justice Programs, National Institute of Justice, 2000. www.ncjrs.gov/pdffiles1/ nij/181867.pdf.

Tödt, Heinz-Eduard. "Theological Reflections on the Foundations of Human Rights." *Lutheran World* 24, no. 1 (1977): 46-58.

Trafficking in Persons Report. Washington, DC: US Department of State, June 2005. www.state.gov/g/tip/rls/tiprpt/2005/46606.htm.

Uddin, Sohel. "Bangladesh Factory Collapse: Why Women Endure Danger to Make Clothes for the West." *NBC News*, May 26, 2013. http://worldnews

.nbcnews.com/_news/2013/05/26/18447688-bangladesh-factory-collapse
-why-women-endure-danger-to-make-clothes-for-the-west?lite.

United Nations General Assembly. *The Convention on the Elimination of All Forms of Discrimination Against Women (CEDAW)*. New York: United Nations, 1979.

United States Senate. *Violence Against Women, A Majority Staff Report*. 102nd Congress, Committee on the Judiciary. October 1992.

Vienna Declaration and Programme of Action. Geneva: Office of the High Commissioner for Human Rights, 1993. www.ohchr.org/EN/ProfessionalInterest/Pages/Vienna.aspx.

Walker, Lenore E. *The Battered Woman*. New York: Harper & Row, 1979.

Watson, Philip S. *Let God Be God! An Interpretation of the Theology of Martin Luther*. London: Epworth Press, 1947.

Williams, Holly. "Survivor of Bangladesh Factory Collapse Speaks Out." *CBS News*, May 23, 2013. www.cbsnews.com/8301-18563_162-57586001/survivor-of-bangladesh-factory-collapse-speaks-out/.

Wind, Renate. *Dietrich Bonhoeffer: A Spoke in the Wheel*. Grand Rapids: Eerdmans, 1990.

Women in Workforce. Washington, DC: United States Census Bureau, 2010. www.census.gov/newsroom/pdf/women_workforce_slides.pdf.

World Bank. *World Development Report 2012: Gender Equality and Development*. Washington, DC: World Bank Publications, 2011.

World Health Organization. *Female Genital Mutilation: Fact Sheet No. 241*. Geneva: WHO, February 2010.

———. *Multi-Country Study on Women's Health and Domestic Violence Against Women*. Geneva: WHO, 2005.

———. *UNAIDS Report on the Global AIDS Epidemic 2010*. Geneva: WHO, 2010.

———. *Violence Against Women: Fact Sheet No. 239*. Geneva: WHO, June 2001.

———. *Violence Against Women: Fact Sheet No. 239*. Rev. ed. Geneva: WHO, 2009.

World Vision. "Introducing World Vision Micro." *World Vision*. www.worldvisionmicro.org/downloads/micro/landing/event_kits/pastor_talking_points.pdf.

———. "Sarah's Story." *World Vision*, www.worldvisionmicro.org/success_stories/6.

Xue, Xinran. "Gendercide: The Worldwide War on Baby Girls." *Economist*, March 4, 2010. www.economist.com/node/15636231.

———. *Message from an Unknown Chinese Mother: Stories of Loss and Love.* New York: Simon & Schuster, 2010.

Yllö, Kersti, and Michele Bograd, eds. *Feminist Perspectives on Wife Abuse.* Newbury Park, CA: Sage, 1988.

Zhu, Wei Xing, Li Lu and Therese Hesketh. "China's excess males, sex selective abortion, and one child policy: analysis of data from 2005 national intercensus survey." *BMJ* 338, no. 7700 (April 18, 2009): 920-23.

Subject Index

Finding the Textbook You Need

The IVP Academic Textbook Selector
is an online tool for instantly finding the IVP books
suitable for over 250 courses across 24 disciplines.

www.ivpress.com/academic/textbookselector